Questions About God

And the Answers
That Could Change Your Life

Questions About God

And the Answers
That Could Change Your Life

Pat Boone
Cord Cooper

Lighthouse
Publishing

Questions About God

And the Answers That
Could Change Your Life

Copyright © 2009 by Pat Boone and Cord Cooper

ISBN-13 978-1-935079-13-2

Published by
Lighthouse Christian Publishing
SAN 257-4330
5531 Dufferin Drive
Savage, Minnesota, 55378
United States of America

www.lighthouseebooks.com
www.lighthousechristianpublishing.com

Contents

About the Authors

PAT BOONE

For five decades, Pat Boone has been a noted figure in the entertainment business. As a recording artist in both the popular and gospel music genres, he has sold more than 45 million units worldwide. As he approached his 50th year in show business, *Entertainment Weekly* hailed him for his 61st hit, "Under God," a top 15 single on Billboard's Hot 100 chart, from his *American Glory* album. In 2003, he was inducted into the Gospel Music Association Hall of Fame.

Boone's career spans virtually all media, and he's been a vital force since shortly after his college days. A graduate of Columbia University, Boone was the youngest star ever to headline a weekly TV variety series, and he went on to appear in films such as *State Fair, Journey to the Center of the Earth, April Love, The Cross and the Switchblade, The Greatest Story Ever Told*, and many more. His first book, *Twixt Twelve and Twenty*, was the No. 1 non-fiction best seller for two years. His book, *A New Song*, sold over a million copies in hard cover, with millions more in paperback; it has been translated into 17 languages.

Today, Boone continues to influence and inspire fans, industry newcomers, and seasoned veterans alike. A successful entrepreneur, entertainment personality, and humanitarian, Boone's contribution to America's culture has been far-reaching. For more than 40 years, a centerpiece of his life has been sharing a positive message of faith and hope.

CORD COOPER

Cord Cooper is an award-winning reporter whose work has appeared in the *Los Angeles Times, Entrepreneur, Investor's Business Daily*, and on CNNMoney.com, Yahoo News, Yahoo Finance, and Web sites sponsored by the *Boston Herald* and Harvard University, among many others.

With fields of expertise including business, entertainment, and politics, Cooper has profiled figures ranging from Presidents Ronald Reagan and Gerald Ford to Nelson Mandela, Charlton Heston, Tony Bennett, Cameron Diaz, Bob Hope, John Glenn, and many others. He is the author or co-author of three books.

Chapter Outline

Chapter One:
If God Exists, Why Doesn't He Appear Visibly?
The chapter opens with astonishing facts about Earth, our solar system, and galaxy. In a novel twist it lists the chapter title midway through, asking the question above. It follows through with an answer that will surprise skeptics and believers alike.

Chapter Two:
Is Truth Relative, Or Absolute?
This chapter demonstrates that truth is absolute and that absolutes exist—even in Einstein's theory of relativity. In doing so, it lays the groundwork for the search for God.

Chapter Three:
Is the Universe Valid Evidence of God's Existence?
We start with a simulated deep-space journey at the speed of light, then take Hubble-like snap shots of the Milky Way, our local group of galaxies, and the farthest reaches of the universe. We then travel back to the dawn of time, and show—through probabilities and

physical laws—that the universe could not have begun uncaused out of nothing.

Chapter Four:
Were Humans Created to Commune With God?
This chapter opens with a famed neuroscientist who shows how the human brain is hard-wired to communicate with a higher power. We then look at case studies from leading doctors and universities, showing how faith and prayer are two of the most potent forces in medicine. We give an overview of more than 200 studies showing a link between health and faith that spans the boundaries of age, culture, geographic location, and gender.

Chapter Five:
If God Exists, Why Is There Tragedy in the World?
This question is answered in unexpected ways. Readers are in for a surprise.

Chapter Six:
Does the Bible Offer Evidence of Divine Inspiration?
The chapter begins by comparing the exotic creation accounts of ancient cultures with the straightforward

chronology in Genesis, illustrating—in ways even many Christians aren't aware—the amazing parallels between the Bible and science. It turns out that Moses' chronology—from sea life to land mammals—is in basic agreement with science's timeline.

The chapter illustrates how archaeology has verified biblical accounts; offers evidence that Moses wrote the Pentateuch; reveals amazing prophecies fulfilled; and ends showing the credible origins of the Bible.

Chapter Seven:
The Flipside: What Motivates Atheists?

Here we focus on why people reject faith. Included are some frank observations, based on discussions with nonbelievers.

Chapter Eight:
Was Jesus the Son of God?

This chapter includes: evidence that the Gospels were written earlier than previously thought; examples showing how Jesus' teachings prove the fall of man; dramatic evidence of Jesus' prophecies fulfilled; historical non-biblical accounts verifying facts in the Gospels; Old Testament Messianic prophecies fulfilled (with evidence that they refer to Christ and not subsequent Old Testament events); archaeology supporting the Gospels; and compelling evidence of the Resurrection.

A Brief Word

This book does not take sides in the "old Earth vs. new Earth" theological debate. The book uses science's figures and hypotheses—about the formation and age of the universe and planet Earth—to challenge certain concepts on scientists' own turf, and to show how scientific hypotheses, principles, and discoveries conclusively point to evidence of God's existence. When using the pronoun "he" and the pronoun objective "him" in reference to God, the book follows the style of the King James Version of the Bible, lower-casing both. When the co-authors speak individually, they're identified parenthetically.

Chapter One

The First Question? Stay Tuned

Things aren't always what they seem.

As you read this, you probably think you're sitting perfectly still. Yet could anything be further from the truth? Right now, you're moving at four incredible speeds simultaneously. First, you're spinning in an easterly direction at 1,044 miles per hour. That's the speed at which Earth turns on its axis.[1]

Second, you're moving through space at 67,000 miles per hour—the speed at which Earth orbits the sun. Third, you're orbiting the Milky Way's galactic center at 490,000 miles per hour. That's the speed at which everything in the galaxy spins around the Milky Way's center of mass. And fourth, as the universe expands, everything in it is hurtling outward at lightning speed (the speed varies, depending on each object's location). Yet even that's not the end of the story. The expansion rate is accelerating.

Yet look at the book you're reading. Look at every inanimate object around you.

To all appearances, everything is perfectly still.

As Copernicus and Galileo found in challenging centuries of entrenched thought, things indeed aren't always what they seem.

In reading this book you'll embark on a journey that will challenge your thinking and point up possibilities you haven't considered. We'll look at mysteries that have captivated mankind for centuries. We'll also see how faith and fact can intersect without our realizing it.

Above all, we'll look at evidence. Evidence that God not only exists but is knowable.

Evidence

It drives our judicial system. It determines the fate of everyone who stands trial. A shred of forensic evidence can mean the difference between a death sentence and freedom. Eyewitness accounts can determine whether a prosecutor pursues a case or drops it.

Evidence also drives science. It results in new theories, new ways of looking at the universe. Science continually changes, replacing old hypotheses with new ones. It continually refines itself, based on evidence.

Science and our system of justice turn on specific standards for evaluating evidence. We'll use those same standards in considering the evidence for God's existence.

First, a Definition of Terms

If a supreme creator exists, it isn't in the form of a cosmic old man with white hair depicted by artists through the ages. The omniscient, all-powerful force behind the universe is exactly that. An all-powerful force. Interestingly, the Old Testament of the Bible describes the Godhead figure not as a man but in several distinct ways. Among them? God as spirit, God as light. Though known to the Hebrews as Jehovah and Yahweh, his physical descriptions are spirit and light.

To avoid endlessly repeating genderless terms— "intelligence," "spirit," "supreme creator"—we'll often refer to God in this book using the pronoun "he" and the pronoun objective "him." These are simply reference points.

The Search

People by the millions have a vague belief in a supreme

being, yet they don't experience God in their lives and they wonder why. They expect God to reveal himself to them at will—their will. Yet does anything else on Earth occur this way?

If you're out of work, do you lie on your couch waiting for prospective employers to come knocking?

When NASA embraced John Kennedy's goal of landing a man on the moon by the end of the 1960s, did it look for ways to gravitationally pull the moon to us, or did it seek every avenue—including failed attempts along the way—to get astronauts from here to there?

Why should the search for God be any different? Interesting question, isn't it? To find anything on Earth or in the universe, we have to look for it. To find God, we must seek him.

"Look, we're finite beings," you're probably saying. "Knowing God—if he exists—is impossible." Which brings us to a couple of questions:

If God Exists, Why Is It Up to Us to Find Him? Why Doesn't He Appear Visibly?

These are questions man has been grappling with for centuries. And the answer could well lie in human nature.

Picture this scenario for a minute: It is night. Pitch dark. Hundreds of millions of people are either asleep or preparing to go to bed. Suddenly an immensely bright light appears. A light brighter than the sun instantly turns night to day. Sleepily, people approach their windows wondering what in the world's going on. They find that though the light is enormously bright, it can be viewed effortlessly by the naked eye. Instead of heat, people feel an incredible tranquility. As by the millions they peer up at the light, they feel a welcoming, almost overpowering love and sense of well-being. Though no audible sound is heard, everyone inwardly—simultaneously—hears a message in his native language. As the message is spoken, everyone stands transfixed before the light, looking up and looking at each other, everyone instinctively aware the message is being understood en masse.

Meanwhile, on the other side of the world, it's the middle of the day, and the same thing is going on. It's daylight, but the light is five times brighter. The message is being heard everywhere on Earth.

It speaks of love, of seeking God, of trading broken lives for eternal peace. It speaks of a divine love that, if accepted, will forever change life as we know it. It speaks of forgiveness and eternal destiny. Then suddenly, the message ends and the light gradually diminishes.

On one side of the world, darkness returns; it is

again night. On the other side, normal sunlight.

People are dumbstruck. Some identify with the intense light and the love. Others are overwhelmed. Everyone instinctively knows they've been in the presence of God.

Within minutes, it's the only news story on television. The cable news media won't let this one go.

The next day, the world's newspapers are awash in five-column photos and banner headlines. Experts give their opinions as to what happened. Priests, rabbis and ministers are consulted.

The following weekend, churches, synagogues and mosques are packed to the gills.

For days, the appearance of the light is all people are talking about. They trade stories as to where they were when it appeared. What they thought it meant. And whether it would appear again.

Weeks later, people speak of it, but not as intently. The events of everyday life are starting to crowd back in. The big picture of love and forgiveness is being blurred as earthly images again take focus.

As months go by, people speak of it less and less. Sunday services start to thin out. Football gradually resumes its place as a Sunday pastime.

As the phenomenon's first anniversary approaches, there's a slight increase in church attendance. Pundits fill the airwaves recalling what happened. Some psychiatrists are now suggesting it was a case of mass hypnosis. More than a few people on the street question whether it happened at all. Some ask: If God cares about us so much, why doesn't he appear again? In the weeks following the anniversary, church attendance trails off to its pre-phenom levels.

Life settles back to the way it was. A small nation invades another. Terrorists blow up an embassy—200 people are killed. Fourteen months after the light appears, as people crowd around TV sets on Super Bowl Sunday, a breaking-news alert announces the possibility of war.

Life on planet Earth is back to normal, as if nothing ever happened.

If God suddenly did appear—to deliver a message and prove his existence in the bargain—wouldn't the aftermath play out exactly this way?

Human nature being what it is, God would have to make regular appearances to keep proving his existence, reducing the Almighty to a cosmic baby-sitter keeping 6.5 billion unruly kids in line. And how ridiculous would that be?

Because humans are the way we are—the details of which we'll discuss later—we must be the ones to reach out to God. And if we want to find him, we can.

Making the journey requires a simple yet powerful tool.

An open mind.

Chapter Two

Is Truth Relative, or Absolute?

The fashionable answer? It's relative, of course. Isn't everything relative?

Absolute truth smacks of arrogance. It flies in the face of political correctness. It implies intolerance. Adherence to dogma. The trashing of other people's views. Truth is personal. It's what you believe it to be. But is it really?

If "personal truth" is what an individual feels is true for him, how is that different from opinion? There are such things as personal truths, but let's be real— they are, in fact, opinions. Whether a person is handsome or ugly, whether a comedian is funny or a waste of time, whether a dress is attractive or atrocious—these are opinions, not truths. A majority of people can find a comedian funny, and the absolute truth about that comedian is this: A majority of people find him funny. Whether he actually *is* funny is a matter of *opinion*.

Truths center on facts. Whether the Earth is flat or round. Whether there are other universes. The number of planets in our galaxy that have circular, rather than elliptical, orbits. The answers to these questions represent truths. Absolute truths. We may not know the answers, but the truths are out there, waiting to be discovered.

The point? Truth exists, regardless of our beliefs or opinions.

Here's a small example (from Cord Cooper). Say I'm holding something behind my back and I ask you to guess what it is. You have no idea what I'm holding, and what I have in my hand could be anything. It could be a cell phone. A tennis ball. Anything. What I actually have in my hand is an orange.

You begin to make your guesses, and all of them are wrong. As you run down the list of obvious choices, the orange remains an orange the entire time. It doesn't transform into a cell phone when you guess cell phone. It doesn't become a tennis ball when you guess a tennis ball.

The absolute truth about what I have in my hand is that it's an orange. No matter what you believe about it, it remains an orange.

So it is with everything on this planet and through the cosmos. The Hubble telescope has sent back spectacular images of the universe the way it existed 14 billion years ago. The images have taken 14 billion years, traveling at light speed, to reach us.

That part of the cosmos has probably changed dramatically since the dawn of time. At this moment, it exists in a form unknowable to us.

We can speculate endlessly about it, but that doesn't change the form it's in right now—just as all the guesses you could make about the orange behind my back wouldn't change the fact it was an orange.

Truths remain truths regardless of our level of knowledge. And by definition, those truths are absolutes. The fact that the Earth is round is not relatively true. It is an absolute. Any condition, circumstance, or set of principles can be summarized as an absolute truth. Take Einstein's special theory of relativity. It, in fact, has absolutes, and by extension, absolute truths. Let's start with the speed of light. Einstein said the speed of light is a constant—it remains 670 million miles per hour in relation to everything in the universe. Another absolute? The law for all motion (the statement itself being an example of absolute truth): "The combined speed of any object's motion through space and its motion through time is always precisely equal to the speed of light," physicist Brian Greene says in *The Fabric of the Cosmos*. Though space and time adjust themselves, Greene notes, "they do so in an exactly compensating manner so that observations of light's speed yield the same result, regardless of the observer's velocity." Then comes what Greene calls "a grand, new, sweepingly absolute concept: absolute spacetime."[2]

Though space and time individually are relative, according to the theory, the overarching absolute is spacetime. "Absolute spacetime does exist," Greene said. For this reason, "Einstein did not suggest or particularly like the name 'relativity theory,'" Greene explained. "Instead, he and other physicists suggested *invariance theory*, stressing that the theory, at its core, involves something that everyone agrees on, something that is *not* relative."[3] (Greene's emphasis.)

In the realm of absolutes, truth is the ultimate absolute. It describes "what is." We may not know about it. And because of our lack of knowledge, we may not agree with it. But that doesn't change the fact that it "is."

When Christopher Columbus set out 500-plus

years ago on a western route to India, hoping to find a new world along the way, the continents and islands he found had existed for eons—without the knowledge of the civilized world. The European establishment believed the Earth was flat and the center of the universe. Columbus was part of a minority who thought otherwise.

Regardless of what anyone thought, the planet was round, suspended in space, and it revolved around the sun. Those were—and remain—three of the absolute truths about Earth's existence. Man's speculation, what he believed to be true, was irrelevant. Individuals' "personal truth"—that the Earth was a giant pancake— was of course not true at all.

Every so-called mystery in the universe has facts attached to it. Those facts represent truths. Just because we're ignorant of those truths doesn't make them relative.

Everything in the universe *is what it is*—with or without our knowledge.

So it is with God. The absolute truth about God is this: Either he exists or he doesn't. And if he exists, he by definition is the author of a set of consistent physical laws. Just as the moon doesn't morph into a ball of green cheese the moment some human on Earth believes it's a ball of green cheese, God doesn't constantly reinvent himself to suit puny mankind's conflicting beliefs—any more than the orange behind my back became a cell phone the moment you guessed it was.

God isn't, at one given moment, a spirit who replicated himself in human form, calling on people to love one another and turn the other cheek—and the very next moment a being who delivers 75 virgins to followers who kill their enemies. He doesn't turn into a cumquat just because an affluent cult in Marin County believes he's a cumquat. Constantly morphing himself to suit the beliefs of 6.5 billion people would leave him little time to do anything else. And what kind of sense would that make?

If God—as the author of constant universal laws— exists, he does so in a specific form. And if he exists, he is the ultimate absolute. The ultimate truth. Which brings us again to the point of this book: laying out evidence for God's existence. Not only that he exists, but is knowable.

What is personal truth for you, and what is absolute? Read on.

Chapter Three

Is the Universe Valid Evidence of God's Existence?

Let's take a journey to find out. Ever wonder what it would be like to travel at the speed of light? You're about to take a simulated journey at 670 million miles per hour. Light speed.

If traveling at the speed of light were technologically possible, it would have to be achieved in stages, to prevent G forces from literally crushing you to death. But for our purposes, we'll assume light speed is achieved at the moment of liftoff.

You're now strapped into your seat—atop a payload of 6.1 million pounds, with millions of pounds of solid and liquid propellant—on a Cape Canaveral launch pad. It's T minus zero. And we have liftoff. Traveling at the speed of light, you reach the moon in a fraction over 1.3 seconds. At 1.5 seconds, you're 28,000 miles past the dark side of the moon.

At 2.6 seconds, you're as far away from the dark side of the moon as Earth is from the illumined side. At 2.1 minutes, you've traveled 23.7 million miles, and you zoom past Venus (at its closest point to Earth on its elliptical orbit). At 4.3 minutes, you've traveled 48 million miles as you hurtle past Mercury (also at its closest point to Earth on its orbit).

At 8.3 minutes you've traveled roughly 93 million miles, and you pass the sun. (Forget the fact that you'd have melted from the heat—with the sun's surface temperature being 10,000 degrees Fahrenheit, and its core temperature ranging from 18 to 27 million degrees Fahrenheit. We're talking only speed.)

After passing the moon in just over 1.3 seconds and traveling 93 million miles to the sun in little more than eight minutes, you continue traveling at that speed without letup for 4.4 years—just to reach our second closest star, Alpha Centauri A. [*]

To reach the farthest star visible to the naked eye— in our neighboring galaxy, Andromeda—you'll travel at

---

[*] This is part of the three-star Alpha Centauri system comprising Alpha Centauri A and B and a dwarf star.

that incredible speed for the next 1.5 million years.

And that star is relatively close. Travel at light speed for 5 billion years, and you'll just scratch the surface of the universe.

At a span of 4.4 light years from Earth, Alpha Centauri A is, by comparison, downright "touchable"— at only 25.8 trillion miles away! The exact figure: 25, 848, 247, 439, 139.8. Since traveling at light speed is impossible, let's figure how long it would take to get to AC-A, the sun's nearest neighbor, with the technology we have.

Moving at 35,000 miles per hour—a typical cruising speed of Voyager 1 and 2—it would take 84,306 years to get to our second closest star. Traveling at 568 miles per second—the speed of the Ulysses probe—it would take 86,500 years to get there.

Cruising at the clip of the Concorde—about 1,335 miles per hour—it would take 2.2 million years to reach Alpha Centauri A. And there are more than 10 sextillion stars and 100 billion-plus galaxies in the visible universe. Yet, pathetically, it would take two of NASA's *fastest vehicles*, Voyager 1 and 2—traveling at 35,000 mph—more than 84,000 years just to reach our second closest star. To put that in perspective, the entire length of recorded civilization on Earth, going back to the Sumerians, is less than 6,000 years.

Even at a distance of 26 trillion miles, Alpha Centauri is giving us a break. The average span between stars in the Milky Way is 36 trillion miles.

Betelgeuse and Beyond

If the distance between stars is incredible, their size is mind-boggling.

Let's start with the sun, which is roughly 109 times larger in diameter than Earth (the sun's diameter is 864,000 miles; Earth's is 7,926). If the sun were hollow, thousands of planets the size of Earth could easily fit into it. Seems like a stretch? Picture it for a moment: If the sun were hollow, 109 planets the size of Earth could fit across its center; above and below that row there would be dozens of empty rows—each successively smaller—that additional Earths could fill. Result: thousands of Earths. Yet, the sun is tiny compared to other stars. Some stars are so huge that, if they were hollow, several thousand spheres the size of the sun could fit comfortably into them.

Take the star Betelgeuse—at about 500 light years from Earth. Located in the Orion belt, Betelgeuse is a red super giant some 600 times larger than the sun. Its *diameter* is roughly 520 million miles, according to the *World Book Encyclopedia*. If Betelgeuse were hollow, the Earth could revolve around our sun *inside the star*.

Earth's orbit around the sun is about 186 million miles in diameter (as opposed to circumference)—so Earth's orbit inside Betelgeuse would be a breeze, with room left over for a duplicate Earth to orbit a duplicate sun, and more than 140 million miles to spare. Put another way, the distance from Earth to the sun comprises less than 20 percent of Betelgeuse's diameter.

In addition to the amazing size of stars is their sheer number. We'll explain how we got our estimated number of stars mentioned earlier. There are more than 100 billion galaxies in the visible universe—each averaging 100 billion stars, according to scientists. One hundred billion galaxies times 100 billion stars equals 10 sextillion—or 10 followed by 21 zeroes. That's the estimated number in the *visible* universe.

Closer to Home

Spanning 100,000 light years, the Milky Way[*] belongs to what astronomers call the Local Group of galaxies—three large and more than 30 small galactic systems. In this group our galaxy is second in size to Andromeda.

With a diameter of three million light years, the Local Group is part of the Local Supercluster—which spans 100 million light years end to end.

---

[*] Though one of the larger galaxies in the Local Group, the Milky Way is average in size overall, containing 100 billion stars.

Traveling at 186,000 miles per second (the speed of light), it would take 100 million years to travel the span of this group of galaxies.

Our Solar Backyard

Located in the outer regions of the Milky Way, our solar system not only stretches across billions of miles, but is larger than previously thought. In November 2003, a planetoid of rock and ice was discovered some 8 billion miles from Earth (representing its average distance from us on its orbit). Given the name Sedna and located beyond Pluto, the planetoid's orbit loops out as far as 84 billion miles from the sun at its farthest point.

Over the last several years, a number of similar planetoids have been discovered beyond Pluto. The growing number caused the International Astronomical Union to downgrade Pluto to a dwarf planet in 2006. Among the reasons: Pluto and its neighboring planetoids (as they were originally classified) were comparably sized. They've since been renamed "plutoids."

Because of their orbits, the plutoids extend so far out in the solar system that, from their vantage point, the sun could be blocked out with the head of a pin. In our neck of the woods, the sun radiates enough heat and light to sustain more than 2,000 Earths. Every second, nuclear fusion in the sun's core converts roughly 700 million tons of hydrogen into about 695 million tons of helium. To put that in perspective, the biggest man-made explosion on record was 60 megatons, or 60 million tons.

Our solar system's former ninth planet—the "recently dwarfed" Pluto—orbits the sun once every 248 Earth years. Since Pluto was discovered in 1930, it's only completed about 27 percent of its current orbit. It will finish that orbit on September 3, 2178.

Though formed about 4.6 billion years ago, our solar system has only orbited the Milky Way's galactic center about 20 times—despite an incredible orbiting speed of 490,000 miles per hour.

With billions of galaxies, satellite galaxies, solar systems, planets, and moons all on their own orbits, it's little wonder that Webster's New Collegiate Dictionary defines *cosmos* as "an orderly harmonious systematic universe." That seems a mastery of understatement.

Planets move with such amazing precision that scientists can predict their paths thousands of years into the future. Galaxies orbit with equal precision (again, orbiting their centers of mass).

But for mind-boggling complexity, we need look no further than planet Earth, home to more than 30 million species, of which only 1.6 million have been named, according to Harvard biologist E.O. Wilson in his book, *Earth's Biodiversity*. The 30-million figure is just an estimate, he emphasizes. The total number of species could reach 100 million and beyond.

The Walking Universe: A Quick Tour

If the human body is one of the planet's more complex organisms, a universe all its own, the human eye is a wonder of intricacy—with six million "cones" to process color vision and 120 million tiny rods for black-and-white vision.

Just as amazing is the human ear, with roughly six million components, by recent estimates.

The average human heart beats about 37.9 million times a year, pumping blood through 62,000 miles of blood vessels—that's about two and a half times the circumference of the Earth. Yesterday your heart beat roughly 104,000 times, sending blood through your system at lightning speeds (the rate varying by location within your body and the type of blood vessel through which it's traveling). During that same 24-hour span, your body produced more than 172 billion red blood cells.

Add to this a possible 100 million other species (98.4 percent of which are unnamed), include uncharted ocean floors and a rock-and-molten netherworld below Earth's surface, and you have a planet that's as far from full discovery as the cosmos itself.

Compelling Evidence

In the last 20 years, as discoveries have unfurled more evidence of complexity in the universe and here on Earth, a number of scientists have taken a second look at the notions of design and an intelligence behind the cosmos.

The July 20 1998 cover of *Newsweek* declared, "Science Finds God." The cover story centered on a conference attended by hundreds of scientists and theologians who concluded that science and religion are finding common ground.

Said South African cosmologist George Ellis, who attended the conference: "There is a huge amount of data supporting the existence of God. But how do we evaluate it?"

Newsweek reported that "for a growing number of scientists . . . discoveries offer support for spirituality and hints at the very nature of God. Physicists have stumbled on signs that the cosmos is custom-made for life and consciousness."

In its April 7, 1980, edition, *Time* magazine ran a

story focusing on compelling evidence of super-intelligent design in the complex arrangement of atoms, the genetic DNA code, the very universe itself. According to *Time*: "In a quiet revolution in thought and argument that hardly anyone would have foreseen only two decades ago, God is making a comeback. Most intriguingly this is happening . . . in the crisp intellectual circles of academic philosophers."

In April 1997, the science journal *Nature* released a survey focusing on the religious beliefs of leading American scientists. Forty percent of the physicists, mathematicians and biologists polled said they believe in God.

Mechanistic (or naturalistic) evolutionists remain unconvinced. For them, the universe's origins are cut and dried. The cosmos and life on Earth formed through undirected, random means. Matter exploded and set the universe in motion. But the questions remain: Where did that matter come from? And how long did it exist prior to the big bang?

Do the Origins of the Universe Point to a Source?

According to naturalistic scientists, the universe began when matter appeared from nothing and exploded, or when matter that always existed suddenly exploded. In either case, they say, the appearance of matter and the explosion that followed came about through random, undirected means.

This one defining moment is interesting because it stands in contrast to everything else we know about the universe. Why?

Everything in science, everything in the universe, has a source. Everything we know on Earth has a source.

But when it comes to the singularity that produced the universe, science says that 1) something came from nothing and exploded, or 2) a particle that always existed spontaneously exploded. In either version, the big bang was the result—without cause.

The problem clearly is not with the big bang. The problem is with the scenarios leading up to it.

Let's look at them more closely.

First, something came from nothing. When in science has this ever occurred? How does something materialize out of nothing? It's a phenomenon that mechanistic evolutionists describe as "unique."

It is indeed unique, because everything else in the universe—from galaxies to quarks—can be sourced except this one defining moment. And it's this singularity on which the theistic-mechanistic debate hinges—an intelligence behind the universe versus random chance.

According to physicist Victor Stenger, a professor at the University of Hawaii, the particle that appeared from nothing shared the same properties as the cosmic void. Thus, he says, its sudden appearance was explainable. Though Stenger is a respected scientist and teacher, a number of his peers—themselves naturalistic evolutionists—say this is mere speculation. Why? Let's look at his statement again.

He says the particle that appeared from nothing shared the same properties as the cosmic void. Only problem? If nothing existed prior to the big bang, as most random evolutionists claim, how could "properties" of any sort be in play? Since the particle can't be explained by shared properties, where did it come from?

This brings us back to square one in our first big bang scenario. How could something materialize from nothing?

In the second scenario, a particle that always existed suddenly exploded. Where did that particle come from? What was its source? How is it possible that that particle always existed?

Scientists who buy the idea that a particle could always exist question how God could always exist. Since a creator-God would by definition create space and time, that creator would exist on a plane apart from both. According to theologians, God is eternal.

But a particle existing forever without cause? What was its source? The particle cannot be God, because mechanistic evolutionists take God out of the equation.

So here we are, left with science's two scenarios: something that came from nothing or a particle that always existed, both totally without cause. In an essay based on a chapter from his book, *The Unconscious Quantum: Metaphysics in Modern Physics and Cosmology*, Stenger lays out his case for random, uncaused processes, including life on Earth. But interestingly, the more he tries to build his case, the weaker his argument becomes.

According to Stenger, "complexity sufficient for life could readily have emerged naturally in [Earth's] primeval chemical stew."

Now consider the probability of that happening—from the noted astronomer Sir Fred Hoyle. He calculated the odds of DNA—the code on which life depends—assembling by chance in Earth's primeval mix. Hoyle found that the probability of DNA assembling randomly is one chance in $10^{40,000}$. That's 10 to the $40,000^{th}$ power, rendered with a 1 followed by forty thousand zeros. Why are the odds so great? Because of the complexity of DNA, and the fact that there are more than 2,000 enzymes.

Stenger agrees with Hoyle's calculation. But, he says, "DNA did not assemble purely by chance. It assembled by a combination of chance and the laws of physics," which materialized within seconds of the big bang.

"Without the laws of physics . . . life on Earth as we know it would not have evolved in the short span of [4.6] billion years. The nuclear force was needed to bind protons and neutrons in the nuclei of atoms; electromagnetism was needed to keep atoms and molecules together; and gravity was needed to keep the resulting ingredients for life stuck to the surface of the earth."

The odds against that complex set of needs being filled randomly are enormous. So are the odds against a universe like ours materializing without cause.

Mathematician Roger Penrose calculated the odds of a universe like ours occurring randomly. According to Penrose, the probability of our universe coming into being—with its enormously complex combination of physical properties—is one chance in $10^{10^{123}}$. That's 10 to the 10th power to the 123rd power, a number so huge it's almost beyond comprehension.

Why are there such huge odds against a universe like ours existing?

A wide range of forces—including gravity and expansion—had to be precisely balanced at virtually the moment of the big bang, or the unfolding starscape would have imploded eons ago, as physicist Stephen Hawking vividly describes:

"If the rate of expansion one second after the big bang had been smaller by even one part in a hundred thousand million million, the universe would have recollapsed before it ever reached its present state."

Theoretical physicist Paul C.W. Davies explains the universe's expansion rate this way:

"Careful measurement puts the rate of expansion very close to a critical value at which the universe will just escape its own gravity and expand forever. A little slower and the cosmos would collapse, a little faster and the cosmic material would have long ago completely dispersed. It is interesting to ask how delicately the rate of expansion has been 'fine-tuned' to fall on this narrow dividing line between two catastrophes."[4]

All of which just begins to explain why Penrose's amazing calculation above is correct. Physicist Victor Stenger doesn't dispute Penrose's calculation any more than he does Hoyle's. Instead, Stenger says this: "Neither Penrose nor anyone else can say how many of the other possible universes, formed with different

properties, could still have led to some form of life."
Note that Stenger is doing two things here: He's
shifting the argument away from our universe and its
complex constants to "other possible universes" (for
which there's no evidence), and then he's saying those
"possible universes" could "still have led to some form
of life."

Some form, perhaps—but not the complex forms
comprising the 30 million-plus species here on Earth
(read Hoyle's calculation above) or a universe with our
delicately balanced constants and properties (read
again Penrose).

The notion of other universes only makes questions
of origin all the more compelling. If there are other
universes, what caused the first of them to exist? Just
as our universe had a beginning—the big bang—other
universes would come into being at specific points in
time or boundaries of time. What brought them into
being?

Stenger has devised computer models showing
what he says other universes might look like. Some of
his models, he says, are shown to produce life forms—
"albeit admittedly strange ones," he concedes.

By contrast, our known universe is staggeringly
majestic. "The odds against a universe like ours
emerging out of something like the big bang are

enormous," said physicist Stephen Hawking.

"The laws of science, as we know them at present, contain many fundamental numbers, like the size of the electric charge of the electron and the ratio of the masses of the proton and the electron. . . .The values of these numbers seem to have been very finely adjusted to make possible the development of life," he says.

"If one considers the possible constants and laws that could have emerged [from the big bang], the odds against . . . life like ours are immense."

Back to the Future

(If the following section is too technical for your taste, skip to page 47: "Can Science and Faith Intersect?" We recommend you at least skim the following passage, since it covers one of the main points of the book.)

Despite the odds against random causation of the universe and life on Earth, mechanistic evolutionists persist. On the origin of time, for example, Stenger says: "One cannot ask, much less answer, 'What happened before the big bang?' Since no time earlier than the Planck time can be logically defined, the whole notion of time before the big bang is meaningless."

In a later essay, "Has Science Found God?"—which led to his book of the same name—Stenger contradicts himself, saying, "Good science practice demands that everything be open to question, including the premises that are used when interpreting data."

If everything should be open to question, why not a cause of the universe that was *coincident with* the big bang?

The term "coincident with" is important when looking at evidence of design versus undirected means.

Since the big bang "produced" time and space, the explosion technically wasn't an "event" at a given point in time, scientists say. Instead, the big bang was the boundary of time, and it is referred to as a singularity. Stenger and other physicists say that since time didn't exist before the big bang, discussing what happened prior to it is meaningless, including its cause. Thus discussing a creator-God as the cause is also meaningless, they say. Yet these same physicists believe that matter sprung into being from nothing before the big bang, so there's an *a priori* occurrence right there.

The time issue is simply an escape hatch for those purporting naturalistic evolution. If an intelligence initiated the big bang, that action would be coincident with the explosion and occurrence of spacetime, not prior to it, says professor William Lane Craig, who holds Ph.Ds from the University of Birmingham in

England and the University of Munich in Germany.

In other words, says Craig, the big bang and its cause occurred at the same time (such an occurrence is called simultaneous causation). This is not to say that a creator-intelligence came into existence with the big bang. Rather, that intelligence brought the big bang's causal elements into being at the same time as the big bang itself. A creator-God initiating the big bang and spacetime—front-loading the values and constants into the singularity—would by definition exist on a plane *apart from space and time.*

University of Pittsburgh professor Adolf Grunbaum, a naturalistic evolutionist, disagrees with Craig. He claims such an occurrence would make cause (the initiator) and effect (the big bang) impossible to differentiate. Grunbaum's reasoning makes little sense and rests on a fake dilemma, Craig asserts. An intelligence-creator would by definition be the cause and the big bang the effect, he says.

Simultaneous causation is not uncommon. Scientists and philosophers—the latter including Immanuel Kant—have often cited examples of it. Kant's classic citation: A heavy ball resting on a cushion. In this case, two things are happening at once. The ball is resting on the cushion, and there's a depression in the cushion. Is there any question as to which is the cause and which is the effect?

Grunbaum doesn't deny the possibility of simultaneous causation. He argues against it occurring at the moment of the big bang. He says that for simultaneous causation to be possible we must have a generally accepted criterion for discerning causes. Only problem? Causes exist whether or not we're able to explain or enunciate them, Craig says. "Grunbaum has not suggested any incoherence or difficulty in simultaneous, asymmetric causation; if there are such causes in the world, they do not have to wait around for us to discover some criterion for distinguishing them."[5]

We don't need a criterion broad enough to cover all possible causes, Craig notes. "All one needs is a way of distinguishing cause from effect in the specific case," he said. The theistic argument presents "a logically airtight means of distinguishing cause from effect. It is metaphysically impossible for God to be caused by the world, since [as initiator] he exists necessarily, whereas the world's existence is metaphysically contingent."[6]

Craig summarizes another of Grunbaum's arguments against the big bang being caused:

1. Only events can qualify as the momentary effects of other events or of the action of an agency.

2. The big bang singularity is technically a non-event.

3. Therefore, the singularity cannot be the effect of any cause in the case of event causation or agent causation.

Craig deftly shows how Grunbaum's argument fails, focusing on item No. 2. "The initial cosmological singularity [the big bang] is causally linked to later spacetime points and events, so that in this case we have events that are the momentary effects of a non-event," Craig says. This disproves Grunbaum's first statement, he notes. "Now consider the final cosmological singularity [implosion] in a universe caught in gravitational self-collapse: Here we have a case in which a non-event is the momentary effect of other events." This also contradicts the first statement. The conclusion in No. 3, then, is based on a false premise (No. 1).

Finally, Grunbaum argues against the big bang's simultaneous causation based on his belief in the B-theory of time. It states that events are "tenseless" and occur earlier than, simultaneous with, or later than other events, and that the distinction between past, present, and future is subjective.

The A-theory of time states that the distinction between past, present, and future is objective. It holds that there are "tensed facts about the universe, and temporal becoming is real, the future being a realm of unrealized possibilities," Craig notes. "Events do not tenselessly subsist; rather they elapse, and things come into being and pass away."

It is called the A-theory of time presumably because it is predominant—the one most of us subscribe to—and for good reason. It clearly makes the most sense. Things do, in fact, come into being and pass away. From stars to humans.

Arguments in favor of the A-theory—aside from basic logic—are that "linguistic tense mirrors the tensed facts that are characteristic of reality," Craig said. "The passage of time is not a myth, but a metaphor for the objectivity of temporal becoming. . . . Temporal becoming is wholly compatible with relativity theory."

The A-theory of time states that things do come into being, including the universe. That returns us to the question of a cause. Take a cause out of the picture—specifically, simultaneous causation—and you're back to this: matter popping out of nowhere.

"Something cannot come out of absolutely nothing," Craig notes. "A pure potentiality cannot actualize itself. In the case of the universe—including any boundary points—there was not anything physically prior to the initial singularity [the big bang]. The potentiality for the existence of the universe could not therefore have lain in itself, since it did not exist prior to the singularity.

"On the theistic hypothesis, the potentiality of the universe's existence lay in the power of God to create it. On the atheistic hypothesis, there did not even exist the potentiality for the existence of the universe. . . I would say that the empirical evidence overwhelmingly confirms the principle that things do not come into existence uncaused out of nothing."[7]

Can Science and Faith Intersect?

Though definitely not a design advocate, Stephen Hawking made this remarkable statement about the universe's beginnings: "I think clearly there are religious implications whenever you start to discuss the origins of the universe. There must be religious overtones. But I think most scientists prefer to shy away from the religious side of it."

Why? Quite simply, because they start with the notion of random, mechanistic origins and then ex-plain all evidence in terms of that model, as Richard Lewontin, a Harvard University professor and evolu-tionist, admits:

"It is not that the methods and institutions of science somehow compel us to accept a material explanation of the phenomenal world, but, on the contrary, that we are forced by our *a priori* adherence to material causes to *create an apparatus of investigation and a set of concepts that produce material explanations*, no matter how counter-intuitive. . . ." (Emphasis added.)

Did an intelligence initiate the big bang?

It's a question Stenger and other mechanistic scientists can't answer. "The most brilliant exposition of the case for evolution will not answer this question," he said, "because it still presumes the pre-existence of laws of physics and values of physical constants that had to be delicately balanced for human . . . life to evolve."[8]

It is precisely that intricate balance—and the enormous odds against it happening randomly—that point to evidence of an intelligence.

God and Einstein

Perhaps the greatest mind of the twentieth century, Albert Einstein recognized that the universe reflected an intelligence behind it. In short, Einstein believed in God. Though Einstein's concept of God was more pantheistic than personal, he nonetheless described God as both spirit and superintelligence.

Read Einstein's words for yourself:

"My comprehension of God comes from the deeply felt conviction of a superior intelligence that reveals itself in the knowable world."

"My religiosity consists of a humble admiration of the infinitely superior spirit that reveals itself in the little that we can comprehend about the knowable world. . . ."

"In view of such harmony in the cosmos which I, with my limited human mind, am able to recognize, there are yet people who say there is no God. But what makes me really angry is that they quote me for support of such views."

"Then there are the fanatical atheists whose intolerance is the same as that of the religious fanatics, and it springs from the same source. . . .They are creatures who can't hear the music of the spheres."

"It is very difficult to elucidate this [cosmic religious] feeling to anyone who is entirely without it."

"Everyone who is seriously involved in the pursuit of science becomes convinced that a spirit is manifest in the laws of the universe—a spirit vastly superior to that of man. . . ."

Chapter Four

The data is startling, the ramifications compelling. According to a report in the Los Angeles Times, *evidence shows the human brain may, in fact, be hard-wired to believe in God. The report details research done by neuroscientist Andrew Newberg, a professor at the University of Pennsylvania. His research leads to an age-old theological question:*

Were Humans Created to Commune With God?

Newberg is a pioneer in the relatively new science of neurotheology, which explores links between the brain and spirituality. His research shows that humans in a meditative state experience a "higher reality," an intense state of awareness he has documented in brain scans.

Newberg's model is based on research begun in the 1970s by psychiatrist and anthropologist Eugene d'Aquili. "D'Aquili's theory described how brain function could produce a range of religious experiences, from the profound epiphanies of saints to the quiet sense of holiness felt by a believer during prayer," Vince Rause wrote in the *Times*.

D'Aquili and Newberg teamed up in the early 1990s, refining and testing the theory. Using imaging technology called SPECT scanning, they mapped the brains of people of faith including Franciscan nuns "engaged in deep contemplative prayer," Rause said. "The scans photographed blood flow—indicating levels of neural activity—in each subject's brain at the moment that person had reached an intense spiritual peak."

Studying the scans, the scientists were drawn to a key orientation area in the brain's left parietal lobe. "This region is responsible for drawing the line between the physical self and the rest of existence, a task that requires a constant stream of neural information flowing in from the senses," Rause wrote.

The scans showed that at peak moments of meditation and prayer, "the [neural] flow was dramatically reduced," Rause reported. "As the orientation area was deprived of information needed to draw the line between the self and the world—the scientists believed—the subject would experience a sense of limitless awareness. . . ."

What d'Aquili and Newberg had captured, Rause said, were snapshots of the brain in a transcendent state of awareness. "These are rare experiences," Rause reported, "requiring an almost total blackout of the orientation area. But Newberg and d'Aquili believed lower degrees of blockage could produce a range of milder, more ordinary spiritual experiences, as when believers 'lose themselves' in prayer or feel a sense of unity during a religious service. Their research suggests that all these feelings are rooted not in emotion or wishful thinking, but in the genetically arranged wiring of the brain."

Rause—who co-authored a book with Newberg called *Why God Won't Go Away*—said his partnership with the neuroscientist began after Rause had been wracked by a series of personal tragedies. In the span of a few years, Rause lost his mother to cancer, his father to heart disease, and also lost four uncles, an aunt, and a grandmother.

"The cumulative effect of all the grief sent me reeling," he wrote. "I tried to find solace in prayer, but the words felt all wrong in my mouth." He tried to rekindle the faith of his childhood, but many years had

QUESTIONS ABOUT GOD

passed. It seemed distant. He recalled how, as he got older, he thought of himself as "a rational guy who had outgrown superstition."

When he needed help the most, though, his rational side fell short. "With middle age encroaching and the universe baring its teeth, I didn't know where to turn. I had fallen into a spiritual no man's land," he wrote.

His literary agent connected him with Newberg, who needed a collaborator for a book on the brain and religion. Passages in the book heightened his awareness, he said. "I can't say I've found religion," he conceded. "But I have come to realize that the biggest, most fascinating mysteries are to be savored, not resolved. And mystery is all around us: We just need to humble our hearts and pay attention."

Faith and Health

If there's evidence showing the human brain is hard-wired to believe in God, several studies link heightened physical resilience to faith in a creator.

"I believe we can prove that belief in God has a beneficial effect" physically, said noted Washington, D.C.-based physician Dale Matthews. "There's little doubt that healthy religious faith and practices can help people get better."[9]

The idea that faith can positively impact human health is not new. What is new is that the health benefits of faith "are becoming the stuff of science," Phyllis McIntosh wrote in *Remedy* magazine.

Matthews and other doctors point to studies in the *American Journal of Medicine*, the *American Journal of Public Health*, *Heart and Lung* magazine, and the *American Journal of Psychiatry*, among many others.

The studies show a dramatic connection between spiritual commitment and longer life, better health, and quicker recovery from illness.

"Whereas factors such as economic status, diet, and exercise have effects on human well-being, religious involvement seems unique in its breadth of influence," Matthews wrote in *The Faith Factor: Proof of the Healing Power of Prayer*.

Reporter Phyllis McIntosh cites a survey of 5,286 Californians in which church members were found to have lower death rates than nonmembers. Dale Matthews points to a similar study of 91,909 people in Maryland's Washington County.

"The study found that those who attended church once a week or more had significantly lower death rates from coronary-artery disease [50% reduction], emphysema [56% reduction] and cirrhosis of the liver [74% reduction]," Matthews said.

McIntosh cites still other surveys. "Those with a religious commitment had fewer symptoms or had better health outcomes in seven out of eight cancer studies, four out of five blood-pressure studies, four out of six heart disease studies and four out of five general-health studies," she reported.

According to Jeffrey Levin, a former professor at Eastern Virginia Medical School in Norfolk, Va., more than 200 studies show a link between health and faith that spans the boundaries of age, culture, geographic location, and gender. The studies found a connection between faith and good health in people of all ages in Europe, the U.S., Israel, and Asia.

Prayer in particular seems to have a dramatic impact. "Prayer evokes beneficial changes in the body," McIntosh said. "When people pray, they experience the same decreases in blood pressure, metabolism, heart and breathing rates as the famous 'relaxation response' described by Dr. Herbert Benson of the Harvard Medical School." But while Benson says the relaxation response works no matter what words are used—it could be any sound or phrase—"those who choose a religious phrase are more likely to benefit" if the phrase is backed by fervent faith, she said.

Perhaps most compelling is a study by cardiologist Randolph Byrd. He divided 393 heart patients from

San Francisco General Hospital into two groups. One group was prayed for by Christians participating in the nationwide study. The other group received no prayer. Patients had no clue as to who was being prayed for and who wasn't.

The study spanned 12 months, with Christians praying for the one group of patients collectively and by name. The group that was prayed for experienced fewer cardiac arrests, a lower rate of congestive heart failure, fewer cases of pneumonia and needed fewer medications including antibiotics.

One noted doctor, Larry Dossey, became so convinced of the power of prayer, he began praying privately for his patients. In several cases he saw unexpected improvement.

And he's not alone. Hospitals and medical schools increasingly are studying the link between spiritual commitment and health. A number of U.S. medical schools offer courses on faith and the human body, and the Mayo Clinic and Harvard Medical School have sponsored conferences on the subject, McIntosh says.

"In a survey of 269 doctors at the 1996 meeting of the American Academy of Family Physicians, 99 percent said they thought religious beliefs could contribute to healing. When asked about their personal experiences," McIntosh said, "63 percent of doctors said God intervened to improve their own medical conditions."

To skeptics who say the faith-health link is attitudinal and a product of the mind, consider this: Studies show that religious faith and, more important, spiritual commitment have a greater impact on health outcomes than mere positive thinking and non-religious meditation.

Recovery Rates

When serious illness strikes, Dr. Dale Matthews said, "religion seems to boost the recovery process significantly."[10] He points to a 1995 study by Thomas Oxman, M.D., of Dartmouth Medical School, which tracked the recovery rates of 232 elderly patients who had undergone open-heart surgery.

"The overall death rate among these patients was 9% in the first six months after surgery. For patients who said they attended church regularly, the death rate was only 5%. The death rate for non-church attendees [almost 15%] was nearly three times what it was for churchgoers," Matthews said.

"More impressive still, within this group of believers, the 37 patients who described themselves as obtaining significant 'strength and comfort' from their beliefs all survived the six-month period," he said.[11]

One link between attitude and health is the immune system. Negative attitudes—from anxiety to feelings of hopelessness and despair—suppress that defense system, which can impact the body in a number of ways, in some cases increasing the likelihood of disease.

The opposite is also true. Positive attitudes help fuel the immune system, helping to fight off disease and spurring recovery rates, especially in cancer patients, studies have shown. Add strong religious belief to the mix, Matthews says, and the immune system appears to work at peak levels. Surveys have shown religious beliefs impact the body positively in other ways as well.

A study of 355 males in Evans County, Ga., showed that those who attended church one or more times per week "had significantly lower blood-pressure readings than individuals who attended church less often. The positive link between church attendance and lower blood pressure held up even when the church attendees were smokers," Matthews explained.

In addition, faith and prayer have helped people overcome a range of obstacles—and later achieve what at first seemed impossible.

Case in point: Roger Crawford. He was born with two deformed legs and no hands—only a thumb and finger at the end of his left forearm, and a thumb-like projection at the end of his right forearm.

Crawford went on to become a high-school tennis champ and a nationally known motivational speaker. He attributes his success to a positive mental outlook—particularly, faith and prayer.

"As I got older, I began to believe more strongly that God gave me my hands and legs for a reason"—to help others overcome obstacles in their lives, Crawford said.

"The power of faith and the power of prayer can help us see opportunities more clearly," Crawford wrote in his book, *Playing From the Heart*.

Is the brain hard-wired to believe in God, as the *L.A. Times* piece suggests? If so, it could explain the power of the mind in overcoming physical setbacks when faith is put into action.

Chapter Five

If God Exists, Why Is There Tragedy in the World?

That's a question millions of people ask, and they often do so to debunk the notion of a good and loving God. If a compassionate God exists, they say, why does he allow tragedy?

Tragedy comes in several forms: natural disasters, man-made (or man-caused) events, and personal tragedies: illness and death.

Let's look first at man-made, or man-caused, disasters.

Most of them, experts say, are preventable. The trick lies in well-targeted observation and quick action, says researcher Kenneth McGee in his book, *Heads Up*.

Below are just three of several man-caused disasters that could have been avoided.

Three Mile Island. In March 1979, a pump used to feed the water supply for steam creation failed in one of TMI's nuclear reactors. "An operator opened a relief valve at the top of the water tank to bring the pressure back to acceptable levels," McGee recalled. The valve should have remained open for 13 seconds but failed to close properly. It remained open for two hours and 22 minutes.

No one noticed.

"The pressure dropped well below the safe operating range, the core of the reactor nearly reached 'meltdown' stage, and a large amount of radioactive material was released into the atmosphere," McGee noted.

The real tragedy? No one should have been surprised the relief valve malfunctioned. "Eighteen months earlier, a similar failing occurred at another reactor (located in Ohio), built by the same company that built the TMI reactors. Babcock & Wilson engineers warned their superiors of the likelihood of the incident occurring at other plants, but no warnings were reported to TMI or any other reactor," he said.[12]

The Space Shuttle Challenger disaster. The explosion in January 1986 was caused by a malfunction in the joint between two lower portions of the right solid rocket motor. "The specific failure was the destruction of the seals intended to prevent hot gases from leaking through the joint during the propellant burn of the rocket motor," a presidential commission reported. Compounding the tragedy? The fact that the failure was expected—due in part to the cold temperatures at the time of launch. Knowing the risks, NASA proceeded with the launch anyway.

9/11. The attacks on the World Trade Center and Pentagon on Sept. 11, 2001, could have been avoided had U.S. government officials in both parties been more vigilant. Had the U.S. captured Osama bin Laden when it had the chance in the late 1990s, after multiple al-Qaida bombings of U.S. interests—and had we tightened airport security when a warning of possible airliner hijackings surfaced in the summer of 2001—the 9/11 tragedy most likely would never have occurred.

Virtually all man-caused disasters could be averted, or their effects drastically reduced—including world hunger.

Doubt it? The Web site of a respected relief organization, www.mazon.org, has declared hunger as "one of the world's most devastating—and most preventable—problems."

There's nothing magical about the soil in America's Midwest. Equally fertile soil is found around the world, frequently in nations where poverty is rampant.

Many of those countries are ruled by despots, who use the supply of food and other means to retain their power. Just one of many examples? Robert Mugabe, head of Zimbabwe in southern Africa. Zimbabwe has some of the most fertile soil in Africa—and has long been known for its farming industry. Mugabe has confiscated the land from many farmers in a bid to retain control of his government. What could be a thriving country has been reduced to a Third World nightmare. Over the decades, similar scenarios have played out in nations throughout Africa.

When drought has hit parts of the continent, charitable organizations throughout the world have stepped in, sending food to the needy. But that food often hasn't reached them. The food supply has been blocked either by opposing factions or government officials in those nations.

Is that God's fault, or is it due more to the weaknesses of mankind?

One of the world's largest cities, Cairo, lies in the Sahara desert. Yet it's one of the most prosperous cities in Africa. Why? Its people have maximized the fertile soil of the Nile delta, and have used commerce and technology effectively to import what they need.

Yet in other parts of the world, including Africa, ample land is available for the growth of food. And man has gotten in the way.

Is that God's fault?

Let's take a look at natural disasters. Virtually all species on Earth have been given natural forms of protection that help them ward off—or at least give them a fighting chance against—predators and the elements. Despite a range of natural disasters that strike our planet, most species survive quite well.

What form of protection has man been given? His brain—his intelligence. The question is: Does he use it? Let's look at natural disasters and see how man has reacted to them.

Hurricanes. What we often term natural disasters are simply earthly processes that perform vital functions. Hurricanes play a vital role in helping to steer weather patterns, and they also clean the oceans, according to meteorologists. When they strike land, they of course can be deadly. However, they usually hit the same bodies of land, making their occurrence unsurprising and somewhat predictable. And how does man react? Let's take a look.

In the U.S., the areas most often hit include the

northern Gulf Coast, Florida, and southeastern states above Florida. In terms of exposure to hurricanes, these are the highest-risk areas in the country. And how does man utilize his form of protection—his brain? Through promotion, tourism, and the endless search for a buck, he makes Florida one of the most populous states in the Union.

When building a city on the northern Gulf Coast—New Orleans—he constructs half of it below sea level, fortifying it with levees. That process continues long after the hurricane risks are fully known. When the levees start to deteriorate due to age, man does little to restore them. Then comes Hurricane Katrina, and people start asking, "If God exists, how could he let this happen?"

When storms such as Hurricanes Charlie and Andrew hit Florida—whose high-risk real estate is dotted with mobile home parks (hello?)—people ask the same question. Shouldn't the question be: "If man has a brain, why does he put himself in harm's way?"

Arizona and Colorado are relatively disaster-free. Yet they're hardly the most populous states in the Union. People would rather have fun in the Sunshine State—and Southern California.

Which brings us to our next natural disaster:

Earthquakes. Cities across Southern California sit precariously atop a complex series of faults, the biggest of which is the San Andreas. That fault is the dividing line between two huge tectonic plates.

Los Angeles and several cities in the neighboring Inland Empire lie on the Pacific plate. Palm Springs, California, and points east are on the North American plate.

Southern California is considered by seismologists as one of the "hot spots" on the so-called Pacific ring of fire. The region's earthquake risks have been known for decades—while people by the hundreds of thousands have continued to flock there.

When the long-expected "Big One"—a huge quake epicentered on the San Andreas—finally strikes, will the resulting disaster be God's fault, or man's? No one forced over 10 million people to crowd into Southern California, while fully aware of the risks.

Like hurricanes, earthquakes perform a function— they relieve the tension around fault lines and bordering tectonic plates. In addition to the benefits cited above, hurricanes, when they hit land, often benefit local ecosystems, clearing overcrowded forests, and allowing the emergence of new trees and other vegetation, according to meteorologists.

We call hurricanes and earthquakes natural

"disasters" because—as a result of our own choices—we're in their path.

You're probably thinking: "Well, there are disasters almost everywhere—you can't run from life." First, we're not advocating running from life—just a better utilization of man's brain. Second, there are many areas that are relatively disaster-free. But people choose not to live there.

Is that God's fault?

Personal Tragedies: Illness and Death

Death is a part of life. But here again, many illnesses and premature deaths are man's fault, not God's. People continue to smoke, knowing full well the risks of getting cancer, heart disease, and emphysema. People drive under the influence of drugs or alcohol, killing or maiming themselves and others. Are these the best uses of the brain man was given?

Yes, some tragedies are unexplainable and seem totally unfair. But are they God's fault?

Many unexplainable tragedies involve some of the factors above. When an innocent child is killed by a drunken driver, is that the fault of a higher power, or the drunken driver?

Some might say, "Well, God could've stopped him." If God were to stop every man-caused accident, he'd have little time for much else. We'd be reduced to puppets, and God would be reduced to a cosmic puppeteer, metaphorically pulling strings millions of times a day to spare us the consequences of our own bad choices. Those choices are the cause of more human tragedy than any other single factor. In the example above, the child was killed because of a man's bad decision to drink and drive.

Obesity increasingly is becoming a worldwide problem, producing a range of health risks. The problem is at its worst in many industrialized nations—where people are well aware of the risks of a poor diet and overeating. Yet many *choose* to overeat and have poor diets.

When health problems result, is that God's fault?

As we said, there are some tragedies that seem unexplainable. But consider this: Regardless of the problems, misfortunes, and calamities that befall us, God is there, aiding, upholding, and comforting, not only through his Spirit but also in the form of caring men and women, friends, family, doctors, firemen, paramedics—first responders of every sort who offer help when it's needed most.

God doesn't cause tragedy, but he's there for us in good times and bad.

Need more evidence? Keep reading.

Chapter Six

Does the Bible Offer Evidence of Divine Inspiration?

The Bible claims to be the inspired word of God—but does it live up to that claim?

Over periods spanning many centuries, writers of the Old and New Testaments repeatedly speak of inspiration from a higher power.

In Deuteronomy 4:2, God says to Moses—credited with writing the first five books of the Old Testament— "Ye shall not add unto the word which I command you, neither shall ye diminish ought from it." We read in

Jeremiah 1:9: "Then the Lord put forth his hand, and touched my mouth. And the Lord said unto me, Behold, I have put my words in thy mouth."

Isaiah made similar claims, as did Ezekiel: "And thou shalt speak my words unto them" (Ezekiel 2:7). Several other writers and prophets—Daniel, Hosea, Joel, and Malachi among them—claim inspiration from God.

In the New Testament, Paul writing to Timothy says, "All scripture is given by inspiration of God" (2 Timothy 3:16). Other scripture writers say the same thing. Inspiration from God is one of the Bible's most consistent claims.

Yet should we believe the book was inspired simply because the writers said so? Or should we take a closer look?

Perhaps the best way to judge the Bible is to compare it with the beliefs and cosmogonies of other ancient cultures and religions. Do their beliefs offer validity beyond mere acceptance by faith? Are they verified by other sources?

The interesting thing about the Bible? As we'll see in this chapter, even those who aren't so-called "believers" concede the Bible's historical accuracy in key passages, as more archaeological evidence comes to light. Facts once thought incorrect in the Bible have been proven true just recently in archaeological digs. Can other religions' source books, and the works of philosophers from antiquity, make the same claim? In addition, biblical declarations and prophecies written thousands of years ago have been proven true within the last 50 to 500 years.

The cosmological "creation" accounts of ancient cultures have a few basics in common. They depict life on Earth starting out in or near water. But soon they deviate into fanciful flight, in some cases depicting gods at war—with gods "mating" and oceans filled with blood. In short, they embrace the exotic features of myth.

Let's start with the ancient Greeks. In one of their many creation accounts, the gods of Earth and heaven mate and produce the first generation of gods and goddesses. A violent battle ensues among the gods, and before it's all over, the goddess of love and sensuality, Aphrodite, emerges, created from sea foam.

The Babylonian "Enuma Elish" ("Creation Epic") is among the most detailed, but no less fanciful. Tiamat is the goddess of salt water, Apsu the god of fresh water. The two mate (their waters commingle) and Tiamat gives birth to gods and goddesses and eventually to a brood of monsters. A gory battle begins, one of the gods murders Tiamat, severs her body into halves—

and uses the upper half to create the heavens and the lower half to create the earth. The ocean becomes the substance from which the universe is then formed. From there, the account gets ever more fanciful.

The Sumerians believed the boundary between Earth and heaven was a solid (most likely metal) vault. The atmosphere, stars, sun, planets, and the moon lay within the vault, and Earth was flat.

In Amazonian cosmology, birds created man and saved him from annihilation.

The ancient Chinese believed the universe was like a big black egg, carrying the god Pan Gu. When he woke from a long sleep, he broke open the egg. From this egg came Earth and the cosmos. Pan Gu eventually died, and his breath morphed into clouds and the wind, and his voice became thunder. One eye became the moon, the other the sun. His limbs and body became five large mountains and his blood became water. Ancient Hindus also believed their Divine One resided in an egg.

Ancient Egyptians worshiped the god of the rising sun (Khepri or Ra-Harakhte), the god of the midday sun (Ra), and the setting sun (Atum or Horus). Also known as Aten, the sun was believed to be an egg laid daily by Geb, the earth-god. Egyptians had gods and goddesses that represented everything from the moon to the sky and beyond.

Compare these accounts with the biblical chronology in Genesis. Nowhere in the Genesis account does it say Earth is flat, as cosmogonies above do. Nor does it say Earth is supported by a structure, as the ancient Greek and Hindu accounts do. It doesn't claim that man was created before sea life, birds or land animals.

The story in Genesis is straightforward, and the order of creation—written more than 3,400 years ago—is in basic agreement with science. Doubt it? Let's take a look.

The account is told from an earthly perspective, in a way that people three and a half thousand years ago could understand. The first verse of Genesis—"In the beginning, God created the heaven and the earth"—is what we'd today call a thesis statement. The chronology of creation follows. The order given in that first verse—the heavens first, Earth second—is not insignificant. It is, in fact, correct. A good deal of the known universe preceded Earth and its solar system. Note that the verse doesn't say "the earth and the heaven(s)." It easily could have, but it doesn't.

Genesis then describes the void prior to creation ("the earth was without form, and void; and darkness was upon the face of the deep"). Next in the chronology, God initiates creation. Genesis describes the sudden appearance of light, followed by creation of the heavens. (The King James Version's first use of the word "waters" is variously translated by scholars as gases, vapors, or a gaseous mass.) Genesis then describes the creation process on Earth (we'll follow it with science's chronology). According to Genesis, marshes and trees appear, and animate life begins in water. Birds appear, among other creatures, then whales. Note the order: birds first, whales later (we'll come back to both in a minute). The oceans become more abundant with life, as does the earth. The next creatures mentioned are land mammals. A specific example—cattle—is given. Several similar unnamed animals are mentioned. Finally, man is created.

This occurs during different "days," which many scholars say represent epochs of time. Written about three and a half millennia ago, Genesis starts by describing a void and ends with the creation of man.

What does science basically say? The big bang occurred, emitting light, as physicist Brian Greene brilliantly illustrates in *The Fabric of the Cosmos*. The eventual formation of galactic systems also emitted light through the expanding universe. Among trillions of solar systems, planet Earth formed, roughly 4.6 billion years ago. (Stick with us during this next short passage, as key points are made. We list specific periods of development to compare biblical and scientific chronologies.)

About 4.5 billion years ago, the crust of the earth formed.[13] Life developed in lakes and oceans, and the first primitive plants appeared on land (the latter occurred late in the Silurian period, between 443 and 417 million years ago[14]). During the Carboniferous period—354 to 290 million years B.C.—land became dominated by a range of plant life, from early club mosses and horsetails to ferns and trees.[15] During the Jurassic period—206 to 144 million years B.C.—the first bird (Archaeopteryx) appeared.[16]

During the Eocene period—55 to 34 million years ago—the first whales appear, as do early forms of the horse, rhinoceros, camel and other hoofed animals.[17] During successive periods, life forms proliferate. And finally, man appears.

Re-read the six paragraphs above. As you do, compare the biblical and scientific chronologies and their basic similarities.

Referencing Earth, the sun, and moon, Genesis 1: 9-19 describes the creation of our corner of the universe. The Bible's first reference to animate life appears in Genesis 1:20: "And God said, Let the waters bring forth abundantly the moving creature that hath life. . . ." This clearly indicates that life began in lakes and oceans. A closer look gives more information. "And God said, Let the waters bring forth abundantly the moving creature that hath life, and fowl that may fly above the earth."

Birds are referenced in verse 20, whales in verse 21. This is interesting because the order is consistent with science's chronology. Science says birds first appeared roughly 206 to 144 million years ago. Whales appeared 55 to 34 million years B.C. (The secondary references to birds in Genesis—in verses 21 and 22— are in the context of ongoing creation, according to scholars.) Land mammals such as horses eventually predominate—also in basic agreement with Genesis, which references land mammals such as cattle. Finally, according to both science and Genesis, man comes on the scene. The account in Genesis isn't meant as an encyclopedic listing of every life form; it's a broad overview. And interestingly, the order basically agrees with science.

If the Genesis account were both myth and morality play, isn't it more likely it would start with the creation of man, since he's the dominant creature on the planet? Since the Bible says man has dominion over the animals of the earth, wouldn't man as the first creation reinforce that more effectively if Genesis was a myth?

"When Moses wrote Genesis, Jews were just as ignorant of science as Hindus, the Chinese, or the Egyptians; yet here we find a record of creation" similar to scientific accounts of the last 150 years, biblical scholar T.J. McCrossan said. Genesis has the creation cycle beginning with the void and ending with man. Along the way are elements such as the appearance of early sea life, birds, whales, large land-based mammals, and man, in general alignment with science's chronology.

Interestingly, the Bible's agreement with science doesn't end with the creation account. Thousands of years ago, the prophet Isaiah unambiguously indicated the planet is round. Isaiah 40:22, written around 700 B.C., states plainly: "It is [God] that sitteth upon the circle of the earth" (King James Version). The modern-English Living Bible translates it in today's terms: "It is God who sits above the circle of the earth."

Until roughly 500 years ago, man believed Earth was as flat as the entrees at IHOP. Thousands of years ago, Isaiah said otherwise.

Over the centuries many of the ancients believed Earth was suspended on the heads of elephants. Others believed the mythical hero Atlas supported Earth on his shoulders. Virtually no one believed Earth was suspended in space. Yet Job, 3,500 years ago, said the following: "[God] hangeth the earth upon nothing" (Job 26:7; King James Version). Thousands of years before Copernicus and Galileo, the Bible stated unambiguously that the earth is round and suspended in space: "It is God who sits above the circle of the earth," and "[God] hangeth the earth upon nothing."

The sixteenth-century astronomer Copernicus turned science upside down when he proved Earth was not the center of our solar system but revolved around the sun. At first, many resisted the discovery because they felt it contradicted the Bible. But the Bible never claimed the sun revolved around Earth. If anything, the descriptions of Earth in Job, Isaiah, and elsewhere support the notion of a planet that is not fixed in place but part of an expanding cosmos, as you'll read below.

The idea of an expanding starscape is of course central to the big bang theory, which was formulated in the early 1920s, and gained traction among scientists in the 1950s and '60s.

The theory maintains that the universe resulted from a "singularity"—an explosion that propelled gases and matter outward, eventually traversing trillions of miles. This singularity marked the beginning not only of the universe but spacetime, according to science.

Only within the last few years has it been discovered that an invisible force—given various names by scientists—is propelling an accelerated expansion of the universe.

With that in mind let's look more closely at Isaiah 40:22, particularly the last half of the verse: "It is (God) that sitteth upon the circle of the earth . . . that stretcheth out the heavens as a curtain, and spreadeth them out as a tent to dwell in."

Note the use of the word "stretcheth." In this context the verb's in the present tense ("stretches"), indicating an ongoing process. One of the definitions of the verb "stretch," according to Merriam Webster's Collegiate Dictionary, is to "expand."

Let's move to another reference, Isaiah 42:5: "Thus saith God the Lord, He that created the heavens, and stretched them out. . . ." Note the two-part process here. "He that created the heavens, and stretched them out." This verse could have said, "He instantly created the *vast* heavens," but it doesn't. It describes a moment of creation, followed by a process. (The verb "stretch" isn't in the present tense here because of the sentence structure—"created" and "stretched." Just as the verb tense is consistent in 40:22, it's consistent here.) The image of a creator stretching or spreading out the heavens is also described in Job 9:8: "Which alone spreadeth out the heavens and treadeth upon the waves of the sea."

Another reference is found in Psalms 104:2: "Who coverest thyself with light as with a garment: who stretchest out the heavens like a curtain." Again, the image of a process, of a stretching out. In the first chapter of Genesis—for example, Genesis 1:6—we find the word "firmament." The Hebrew word most closely describing "firmament" is "expansion," according to the Cambridge University Press edition of the KJV.

In Genesis, Isaiah, Job, and the Psalms, a creation "process" is described—initiation followed by a stretching out.

Reality Check

We'll now look at the complete text of Isaiah 40:22, and then run the facts regarding life on earth. The verse: "It is God who sits above the circle of the earth. The people below must seem to him like grasshoppers. He's the one who stretches out the heavens like a curtain and makes his tent from them" (Living Bible).

Let's do the reality check. We exist on a small round planet, correct? We're comparatively tiny creatures—one could say that from above, we look like ants or grasshoppers—true? We're part of an expanding universe, which science now says is being propelled by an invisible force. Also true.

Let's look at the verse from two perspectives: with God a part of it, and with God taken out. If we're tiny creatures on a round planet, moving through a stretched or expanded starscape, and God is the omnipresent force behind it all (ruling over and dwelling throughout the universe—as the metaphoric references to "sitting above" and "making a tent from the heavens" indicate), then the verse above is amazingly accurate. But even if you extract God from the verse, you're left with a round planet ("the circle of the earth"), containing small creatures (that seem as small as grasshoppers), moving through a stretched or expanded cosmos ("the heavens" "[stretched] out as a curtain"). The kicker: It was written two thousand seven hundred years ago (circa 700 B.C.).

None of the verses above indicate the vast universe was created as is, in an instant. In all cases a process is described, a consistent image of a stretching out. Written thousands of years ago, the verses defy science's outdated steady-state theory and are more in keeping with big-bang cosmology. As noted, the verses describe initiation followed by process (Genesis 1, Isaiah 42:5); a process marked by expansion (Isaiah 40:22, 42:5; Job 9:8, 26:7; Psalm 104:2); a round planet (Isaiah 40:22) suspended in space (Job 26:7:

"God stretches out heaven . . . *and hangs the earth upon nothing*" [Living Bible]).

Nowhere does the Bible say Earth is flat. Quite the contrary, as shown above. The biblical reference to the "four corners of the earth" is a metaphor for all parts of the planet, just as the earlier reference to God "sitting above" and "making his tent" from the heavens are metaphors for an omnipresent God who rules over, and dwells throughout, the universe. When we say "sunrise" and "sunset," we're obviously not referring to a sun that rises and sets, but rather to an appearance of a sunrise and sunset as Earth rotates.

The writers of the Bible had a clear command of language. They were skilled in the use of literary tools ranging from simile to metaphor and beyond. As an example, see Isaiah 40:15: "Behold, the nations are like a drop from a bucket, and are regarded as a speck of dust on the scales..." (New American Standard Bible). Clearly this is a figure of speech known as a simile.

When a CNN reporter, on the day of broadcaster Peter Jennings' death, said Jennings had covered events "from all corners of the earth," was he literally referring to "corners" of a "flat Earth"? Similes and metaphors have been part of literature for millennia. Like "a drop from a bucket" and "dust on the scales," the biblical "four corners" reference is a figure of speech.

The bottom line? Not only does the Bible *not* say Earth is flat, it describes a round, suspended planet in fairly clear terms.

Let There Be Light

The Bible's references to light are also consistent with science. Thousands of years before the nature of light was known, Job posed this question: "Where is the way where light dwelleth?" (Job 38:19). As biblical scholar T.J. McCrossan noted, the passage doesn't say "Where is the *place* where light dwelleth?" Light travels at 186,282 miles per second. It couldn't possibly dwell in any one place. The Job passage, written over 3,500 years ago, easily could have said, "Where is the place where light dwelleth?"

It didn't.

Thousands of years before scientists knew the speed and nature of light, the Bible posed a question in correct scientific terms.

In 1615 A.D., William Harvey made one of the great scientific discoveries of his era—that blood circulates through a complex network and is the primary agent that nourishes millions of organisms. Blood circulates through all vertebrates; the term *blood* is also used to describe a similar fluid in nonvertebrates. Harvey's discovery identified blood as essential to life. Yet in Leviticus 17:14, written 3,450 years ago, Moses made this statement to the people of Israel: "For the life of all flesh is the blood thereof. . . ." This reiterated his statement several verses earlier: "For the life of all flesh is in the blood." The context was a warning to the Israelites to exclude the blood of animals from their diets. Chapter 17 includes at least three statements about the essential, life-giving nature of blood, each backed up, millennia later, by science.

In the book of Psalms, King David writes a song of praise to God honoring his power. "Their line is gone out through all the earth, and their words to the end of the world. In them hath he set a tabernacle for the sun, which is as a bridegroom coming out of his chamber, and rejoiceth as a strong man to run a race. His going forth is from the end of the heaven, and his circuit unto the ends of it: and there is nothing hid from the heat thereof" (Psalm 19:4-6).

Critics of the Bible claimed this passage incorrectly referred to the sun moving around Earth. Only within the last eighty years have we learned that the sun and our solar system revolve around the Milky Way's galactic center, covering a huge orbit that spans more than 220 million years. The concept of an orbit didn't come into being until the sixteenth century. David used a word translated as "circuit" to describe the sun's path. A dictionary definition of "circuit"? "A usually circular line encompassing an area."

Let's look again at the passage above: "In them hath he set a tabernacle for the sun, which is as a bridegroom coming out of his chamber, and rejoiceth as a strong man to run a race. His going forth is from the *end of the heaven, and his circuit unto the ends of it*: and there is nothing hid from the heat thereof." This describes the sun spanning the heavens on a vast circular journey ("going forth . . . *from the end of the heaven,* and his *circuit unto the ends of it*"). The key words: "*from* the end," "*circuit* [circular path]," and "*unto* (or *to*) the ends." The description—of a vast, repeated orbit—is accurate.

Biblical Prophecy: Fast Forward

Thousands of years ago Daniel recorded the prophecy that in Earth's end times "knowledge shall be increased" (Daniel 12:4).

You're probably thinking, "So what? That's a safe call. Of course knowledge would increase over time." But who could have predicted—thousands of years ago or even 300 years ago—the speed at which knowledge would expand? It's been estimated that man's knowledge from the dawn of civilization to 1750 A.D.

doubled within a span of 150 years—from 1750 to 1900. By 1950, that body of knowledge doubled again. In the following ten years—by 1960—it doubled yet again. And in the years since, man's knowledge has doubled every two years.

The prophecy in Daniel 12:4 is actually two predictions in one: "to the time of the end: many shall run to and fro, and knowledge shall be increased" (KJV). The Living Bible puts it this way in modern English: ". . . the end times, when travel and education shall be vastly increased."

Not bad for 2,600 years ago, when Daniel wrote this prophecy. Is there any question the amount of travel and knowledge increased exponentially during the twentieth century and beyond? In the 1900s, automobiles revolutionized travel. Train travel became more common. Over the next several decades, shipbuilding technology grew more sophisticated. By the 1930s, passenger air travel had become a reality.

The 1950s brought us the Jet Age, which increased air travel worldwide. By the end of the 1960s, man had landed on the moon. In the decades since, as Earth's population has exploded, travel in virtually all its forms has increased unbelievably.

The last 100-plus years have taken us from Model Ts to Maseratis, from steam-belching locomotives to bullet trains, from Kitty Hawk to the International Space Station. We've rocketed from Royal typewriters to the Internet, from steady-state theory to inflationary cosmology and quantum physics. And knowledge continues doubling every two years. ". . . The end times, when travel and education shall be vastly increased. . . ."

From Oppression to Victory

Throughout the Old Testament are prophecies about the Hebrews and their descendants. Case in point? Genesis 15:13-14: "And [God] said to Abram [Abraham], know of a surety that thy seed shall be a stranger in a land that is not theirs, and shall serve them; and they shall afflict them 400 years. And also that nation, whom they shall serve, I will judge: and afterward shall they [the Hebrews] come out with great substance."

As McCrossan, the noted biblical scholar, pointed out, "These words were spoken to Abraham fully 300 years before Joseph was born, and the Israelites were not made slaves in Egypt until long after Joseph's death."

Eventually, Jews were enslaved in Egypt for 400 years, until Moses led them to a land of "great substance," just as had been predicted to Abraham.

Another prophecy is found in Deuteronomy 28:64-66. "And the Lord shall scatter thee [the Hebrews] among all people, from one end of the earth even unto the other. . . . And among these nations shalt thou find no ease, neither shall the sole of thy feet have rest: but the Lord shall give thee there a trembling heart . . . and sorrow of mind: And thy life shall hang in doubt before thee; and thou shalt fear day and night, and shalt have none assurance for thy life."

Is there any doubt that Jews have been scattered to the ends of the earth and persecuted through the centuries? Note that God doesn't say he caused the persecution. He says only that he scattered, or assimilated, the Hebrews.

Masada and Jerusalem

As biblical scholar Peter Gammons notes, the overthrow of Masada and destruction of Jerusalem by the Romans in A.D. 70 brought an end to the state of Israel. Over the next two thousand years, Jerusalem would be overthrown 40 times—by, among others, Mohammad, the Crusaders and the Turks, Gammons notes.

More than 600 years before the destruction of Jerusalem in A.D. 70, Ezekiel predicted the death of Israel, likening it to a corpse of dried bones. He then described a Phoenix-like rise: "These bones are the whole house of Israel: behold, they say, Our bones are dried, and our hope is lost: we are cut off for our parts ....Thus saith the Lord God; Behold, O my people, I will open your graves, and bring you into the land of Israel. . . .Ye shall live, and I shall place you in your own land: then shall ye know that I the Lord have spoken it, and performed it, saith the Lord" (Ezekiel 37:11-12, 14).

For almost two thousand years, Jews clung to the hope that they would return to their homeland, as predicted not only by Ezekiel but also Jeremiah (16:14-15; 31:8-9), Amos (9:14-15), and others.

In the twentieth century, those prophecies were sweepingly and dramatically fulfilled.

The Modern State of Israel

The liberation of Israel had its roots in unlikely—and, some say, miraculous—events. During World War I, Jewish scientist and British subject Chaim Weizmann developed a synthetic acetone to be used in the manufacture of TNT. "Weizmann's discovery came at one of Britain's worst hours during the war and solved the problem of the shortage of acetone for the manufacture of ammunition," Gammons said.[18]

Weizmann's influence shot up exponentially, and he used it to spearhead a move to make Palestine a

Jewish homeland again. On November 2, 1917, British Foreign Secretary Arthur Balfour wrote the following in a letter to Lord Rothschild: "His Majesty's Government view with favor the establishment in Palestine of a national home for the Jewish people, and will use their best endeavors to facilitate the achievement of this object."

British forces later took command of the region, liberating Palestine from Turk rule and paving the way for Jews to return to their homeland. The British occupation of Palestine was given a mandate by the League of Nations in 1922.

The rise of anti-Semitism in Europe in the 1920s, and Adolf Hitler's rise to power in Germany in 1933, caused increasing numbers of Jews to emigrate to their homeland. By 1936, the Jewish population in Palestine had reached more than 400,000, Gammons says. Bowing to pressure from Arab nations, Britain began limiting the number of Jewish immigrants at the very time Palestine's floodgates should have been opened.

As the end of World War II revealed the full horrors of the Holocaust, pressure mounted for the establishment of an independent Jewish homeland. In 1947, Britain turned to the United Nations, which proposed, via special committee, a Jewish state, with Jerusalem under international trusteeship. The plan would have to be approved by the General Assembly.

"On November 29, 1947, Jewish history hung in the balance as the matter came to a vote," Gammons recalled. "Jewish people around the world sat transfixed to their radios during the unforgettable broadcast from the United Nations. The vote, which would seal the end of their years of exile, lasted just three minutes." The result? Thirty-three in favor, thirteen against, with ten abstentions.

Newspapers worldwide bannered the headline, "A Jewish state." Said Golda Meir: "For two thousand years we longed for deliverance. We awaited this great day with awe. Now that it is here it is so great and wondrous that it surpasses human expression." On Friday, May 14, 1948, the State of Israel was established.

David Ben-Gurion read from the Declaration of Independence: "After being forcibly expelled from the land, the people kept faith with it throughout their dispersion and never ceased to pray and hope for their return to it and for the restoration in it of their political freedom. . . ."

Over the next year and a half, more than 350,000 Jews streamed into Israel, recalling the words of the prophet Jeremiah, who predicted, hundreds of years after Moses and the Exodus: "Therefore, behold the days come, saith the Lord, that it shall no more be said, The Lord liveth that brought up the children of Israel out of the land of Egypt; but, the Lord liveth that brought up the children of Israel from the land of the north, and from all the lands whither he had driven them; and I will bring them again into their land that I gave unto their fathers" (Jeremiah 16:14-15).

"...And I will cause them to return to the land that I gave to their fathers, and they shall possess it" (Jeremiah 30:3).

"Behold, I will bring them from the north country, and gather them from the coasts of the earth . . . a great company shall return thither. . . . They shall come with weeping, and with supplications will I lead them: I will cause them to walk by the rivers of waters in a straight way, wherein they shall not stumble: for I am a father to Israel. . . ." (Jeremiah 31:8-9.)

Soon after the establishment of Israel, Prime Minister David Ben-Gurion led an inspirational campaign to make the desert "blossom like a rose." He brought in "thousands of young people to develop the barren Negev," Gammons recalled. "All over Israel new towns and villages began to spring up."

Thousands of years ago the prophet Amos described the restoration of Israel: ". . . and they shall plant vineyards, and drink the wine thereof; they shall also make gardens and eat the fruit of them. And I will plant them upon their land, and they shall no more be pulled up out of their land which I have given them, saith the Lord thy God" (Amos 9:14-15).

"Today, Jewish people from 120 nations, speaking 83 languages, have made the land of Israel their home again" as the Bible predicted, Gammons notes.

"And it shall come to pass in that day, that the Lord shall set his hand again the second time to recover the remnant of his people, which shall be left from Assyria, and from Egypt, and from Pathros, and from Cush, and from Elam and from Shinar, and from Hamath, and from the islands of the sea" (Isaiah 11:11).

"Note the term 'a second time,'" Gammons said. "In this prophecy, made before the Babylonian captivity, the prophet foresees that the Jewish people will not just be scattered from their land and re-gathered once, but twice. He looks beyond the Babylonian captivity and their return to Jerusalem, to a second, far greater scattering and re-gathering," during the period after the fall of Jerusalem in 70 A.D.[19] This is reinforced, Gammons says, by the list of places Isaiah mentions, from what is now modern Iran and Iraq to Ethiopia and beyond.

Soon after the restoration of Israel in 1948, hundreds of thousands of Jews emigrated to Israel from Iraq, Iran, north Africa, Turkey, Yemen, as well as Poland, Bulgaria, Czechoslovakia, and nations throughout the world.

"Behold, I will bring them from the north country, and gather them from the coasts of the earth. . . ." (Jeremiah 31:8.) ". . . The Lord liveth that brought up the children of Israel from the land of the north, and from all the lands whither he had driven them: and I will bring them again into their land that I gave unto their fathers. . . ." (Jeremiah 16:15.)

The Bible and Archaeology
Over the last 150 years, archaeology has proven the Bible accurate on details that had previously been dismissed as myths. The Old Testament book of Second Chronicles, chapter 33, verse 11, says the king of Assyria took the captive King Manasseh of Judah to the city of Babylon. Some critics held that since Nineveh was the capital city at the time, Manasseh would have been taken there. But in 1872, British Assyriologist George Smith discovered tablets at Nineveh that confirmed the biblical account.

Evidence of Moses and the Exodus
The story of Moses, of course, is one of the most familiar accounts in the Old Testament. Some scholars

have claimed the story was made up by Jewish scribes to suit their own theological purposes—written late in Israel's history, between the seventh and third centuries B.C.

But according to a Discovery Channel documentary produced by the BBC, evidence is emerging that sheds new light on the Bible's accuracy.

Part of the problem in uncovering evidence of the story is the huge expanse of the Sinai desert. Intermittent wars in the area have also delayed archaeologists' work. But since the peace accords between Egypt and Israel in the late 1970s, archeologists have resumed excavations that have produced promising results, according to the BBC.

One such site in the Sinai is the mountain of Serabit el-Khadim. Near the top of the mountain is a network of ancient mines, where slaves were brought from throughout Egypt to dig for the precious stone turquoise. Some of the slaves were Semitic, and very likely were Hebrews, evidence in the BBC report showed. Graffiti found on the walls is in Semitic, the language from which Hebrew is derived.

What's so significant about Semitic graffiti? It is evidence that Hebrews were in the Sinai and beyond during the reign of the ancient pharaohs. Until recently, some scholars had mocked the story of Moses because no such evidence of Hebrews had ever been found.

One of the many experts who've been to this Sinai mountain is James Hoffmeier, an Egyptologist from Wheaton College in Illinois. He describes graffiti found on one of the mine's walls: "We have here two letters that read 'El,' which is a Semitic term for God. And then, to the right, there is an adjective describing this God, and it's the word 'Olam,' which means 'eternal.' This is very similar to the names of God that we have in the book of Genesis, where God is referred to as 'El Shaddai,' 'God almighty,' or 'El Elyon', 'God the most high one.'"

The amount of graffiti found on the mountain is remarkable, Hoffmeier and others say, because it stands as evidence that the Hebrews were not only Egyptian slaves but that they could write.

Said Hoffmeier: "The tendency has been to somehow reduce the Hebrews to a subhuman status— that somehow they couldn't have written. [Scholars thought] it wasn't until much later that they developed the scribal skills to record. But if we can find common [slaves] able to etch their names on stone, then surely there was no problem for the Hebrews to record things that were important to them."

The Old Testament story of Moses begins in the

Nile delta, where nomadic Hebrews had settled while searching for water and food. They established settlements, and over time their population grew. They were people of a different faith—dismissed as heretics by Pharaoh's court. The best way to control them, Pharaoh cynically concluded, was to use them as slaves.

Skeptics have claimed there's no evidence of Hebrew slaves in the delta. "But in recording the story," the BBC documentary noted, "the Bible adds small but telling details peculiar to life in the delta, which a later scribe, making the story up in Jerusalem, couldn't have known."

Case in point—Exodus 1:14: "And [the Egyptians] made their lives bitter with hard labor in mortar and bricks. . . ."

Delta houses are still built in the traditional way—from bricks made with mud and water and then allowed to dry. According to the BBC, "It was a common building technique in the Egyptian delta—but not in Jerusalem. Unless a Jewish scribe had an eyewitness account to go by, he wouldn't have picked up on this detail."

"In Jerusalem," Hoffmeier noted, "the architecture is made of stone," not bricks.

Though useful as slaves, the Hebrews were

considered a destabilizing influence in Egypt. According to the Bible, Pharaoh ordered midwives to kill every newborn Hebrew boy, to eventually render the Hebrew population extinct. One mother, though, hid her baby in a basket among the bulrushes lining the Nile. The baby was found by Pharaoh's daughter, who adopted him and raised him in her father's palace.

Some experts have written this off as legend, saying it was copied from a story in Babylon. According to myth, Babylon's King Sargon was also found in a basket in a river. The similarities are scant. For one thing, Moses never became a king. And then there's this, as the BBC reported: "[If the Moses story were copied], then one might expect to find echoes of Babylonian words in the original Hebrew story. And yet there are none. In fact, many of the key words are of Egyptian origin. For example, in Hebrew, the word for 'reed' is 'suph.' The word for 'reed' in Egyptian is also 'suph.' The same goes for other crucial words in the story. The words for 'Nile,' 'riverbank,' 'basket,' and for 'bulrushes' are Egyptian. Even the name 'Moses' is Egyptian. It means 'one who is born'" or drawn out.

"How would a Jewish writer, sitting in Jerusalem in the fifth century, know these Egyptian words? It sounds like someone living much closer to the times, who perhaps was even bilingual," said Hoffmeier.

Moses, raised in Pharaoh's court, would have been bilingual, first speaking fluent Egyptian and later Hebrew—when he realized he himself was a Hebrew.

Archaeologists have verified another detail mentioned in the Exodus account. The Bible says that after Pharaoh released the Hebrews, he changed his mind and sent an army with 600 chariots to stop them. Some scholars have said that while the Pharaohs were known to ride chariots, there was no evidence an army with 600 chariots ever existed.

But in the 1990s in Kantir, the site of Pharaoh's capital city, German archaeologists discovered a tethering stone used to secure horses. Then they found a hubcap for a chariot wheel. What they eventually found was a stable for a horse and chariot.

They continued digging. By the end of their search, they'd unearthed stables for about 500 horses and chariots. Said Dr. Edgar Pusch, the excavation leader and director of Germany's Excavation Center: "This proves scientifically that the large number of chariots described in the [Bible] is actually true, and cannot be dismissed as impossible."

Over the years, critics have charged that someone else wrote the books of Moses, including Exodus. But they ignore an important fact: Moses was raised in Pharaoh's court as the son of Pharaoh's daughter. The

Egyptians had developed a culture advanced in art, architecture, and beyond. By today's standards, a number of scholars assert, Moses would have been given the equivalent of a Harvard education.

He certainly would have been able to read and write—and when he later found he was of Hebrew origin, he would have learned the language of his people. He would have been able to record the events of his life, the exodus from Egypt, and the journey of his people to the Promised Land.

According to the BBC, "The evidence from the graffiti in the turquoise mines [mentioned earlier] suggests that the Hebrews could write. If so, then their chief scribe may well have been the most literate among them—the one educated in Pharaoh's court— Moses himself."

Origins of the Bible

The original documents of the Old and New Testaments were copied by scribes and oracles, sometimes simultaneously. Over time, the copies were copied, "until at last some of those copies came into being which have remained to our own day as the earliest extant biblical manuscripts," according to scholar F.F. Bruce, D.D.[20] "It is, in a way, surprising that so much biblical literature survived the adventures and vicissitudes experienced by the people of God throughout the early centuries. Most if it was written on very perishable material. It was exceptional for any part of Scripture to be incised on stone tablets, as the Ten Commandments were. That we have so many biblical tests from the period before the Babylonian exile approaches a miracle," he said.[21]

History records that the prophets and other authors took great care to preserve their work. "Isaiah, finding that his early messages went unheeded by king and people alike, wrote them down, sealed them, and entrusted them to his disciples, so that when at last his warnings came true the scroll could be unsealed and it would be recognized that he had prophesied truly," Bruce said.[22]

Many of Isaiah's prophecies came true centuries later, including his prediction and detailed description of the coming Messiah. As noted earlier, some of his prophecies have come true in our era, thousands of years after they were first recorded.

Other prophets took equal care to ensure their work was carefully recorded. Jeremiah dictated his prophecies to his personal assistant and secretary, Baruch, who recorded almost 40 years of the prophet's ministry. "In fact, two editions including Jeremiah's later oracles have come down to our day," Bruce said.

Over the centuries, scribes were meticulous in copying the original documents of the Old and New Testaments, Bruce and other scholars point out. The amazing discoveries of the Dead Sea Scrolls in 1947 and beyond attest to the amazing accuracy of the copyists over periods spanning hundreds, and sometimes thousands, of years. The scrolls contained "the oldest surviving copies of Hebrew Scripture, dating from the closing centuries B.C.," Bruce noted.

Prior to the discovery of the scrolls in the Qumran caves and other areas west of the Dead Sea, a cache of Old Testament manuscripts had come to light "with the discovery of the storeroom of the ancient 'Ezra Synagogue' of Fustat [Old Cairo]," Bruce explained. "The hundreds of thousands of literary fragments found in this storeroom, now dispersed in a number of libraries in various lands, include many biblical texts that enable us to trace in greater detail the work of the Masoretes"—Jewish scholars and preservers of masorah ("tradition").

Schools of Masoretes worked on Old Testament Hebrew text starting in the sixth century A.D. They equipped it with an elaborate system of symbols indicating traditional punctuation and pronunciation so that public readers of the Bible "would convey the true sense to their hearers as accurately as possible,"

Bruce said. The oldest such manuscripts belong to the period around A.D. 900.

Imagine the excitement, then, when the Dead Sea Scrolls were discovered, starting in the late 1940s. Dating back more than 1,000 years prior to the Masoretic text, the scrolls showed in amazing detail just how carefully and accurately later generations of text—from the closing years B.C. to around A.D. 900—had been copied.

This is what Bruce has to say about the overall accuracy of the Bible, as evidenced by carefully rendered copies spanning thousands of years. "In regard to their manuscript attestation, the books of the Old and New Testaments are unparalleled among the literature that has come down to us from classical antiquity. Both in the abundance of this attestation and in the relatively short interval separating the earliest manuscripts from the original date of composition, the Bible is incomparably better served.

"If the multiplicity of biblical manuscripts increases the sum total of scribal errors [amazingly low considering the number of copies], it also increases the evidence by which these can be corrected and removed, and gives us all the confidence we could desire that the text of Holy Scripture has been preserved in its integrity from the beginning to our own day."[23] As noted, the overall accuracy of copies through the years was proven with the discovery of the Dead Sea Scrolls.

For the study of the Bible, Bruce says, the most important of these scrolls were found in eleven caves at Qumran, northwest of the Dead Sea. These manuscripts are believed to have come from the library of a Jewish religious community that had been headquartered in the area for about 200 years, until the Jewish revolt against Rome—which began in A.D. 66 and ended with the destruction of the Temple and city of Jerusalem in A.D. 70, Bruce notes. A second set of scrolls came from caves farther south, near the west shore of the Dead Sea.

Included among the scrolls was the entire book of Isaiah in Hebrew, "centuries older than anything of the kind previously known," Bruce recalled. Scholar W.F. Albright proclaimed it "the greatest manuscript discovery of modern times. And there cannot be the slightest doubt about the genuineness of the manuscript." Albright's judgment has since been confirmed by a range of experts.

"Scholars in general had discounted the possibility of ever finding biblical Hebrew manuscripts of such antiquity. But now a gap of a thousand years in the textual history of the Old Testament had been most unexpectedly bridged," Bruce said.

"In the Qumran caves over 100 copies of Old Testament books have been found in the original Hebrew or Aramaic text. Most of these have survived only in fragments, but a few copies are reasonably complete. From Cave 1 there is the great Isaiah scroll; from Cave 11 are copies of Leviticus and the Psalms in relatively good condition. All 24 books of the Hebrew Bible [corresponding to the 39 books of our Old Testament] are represented among the Qumran discoveries with the exception of [the book of] Esther," Bruce said.

"From or near Murabba'at, Hebrew fragments of Genesis, Exodus, Numbers, Deuteronomy, and Isaiah have been recovered, and a preserved roll of the Twelve Minor Prophets. The caves of the Wadi Heber, near En-gedi, have yielded Hebrew fragments of Exodus and Psalms. From Masada have come Hebrew fragments of Leviticus [and] Psalms. In addition to pieces of Hebrew scripture, the caves have provided us with some fragments of the Greek translation of the Old Testament, commonly called the Septuagint. Septuagint fragments of two manuscripts of Leviticus and one of Numbers have been identified from Cave 4 at Qumran; Cave 7 has yielded Septuagint fragments of Exodus."24

But the most important Septuagint discovery in the

Dead Sea region is a fragmentary copy of the Minor Prophets in Greek, "exhibiting a text in agreement with that cited in the writings of Justin Martyr, in the middle years of the second century A.D.," Bruce said. "It has been hailed as a 'missing link' in the history of the Septuagint text."

The scrolls greatly expanded scholars' knowledge of the history of Old Testament text. Scroll fragments and in some cases complete books have helped scholars trace a consistent pattern of meticulous copying of biblical text going back thousands of years. They indicate a pattern of scribal accuracy—in copying books of the Bible from generation to generation— going back to antiquity.

The scrolls "make it plain that the text which was standardized by Rabbi [Ben Joseph] Aqiba and his colleagues about A.D. 100, the text that passed through the hands of the Masoretes, and is basic to all the principal versions of the English Bible, was the most accurate type of text available either then or subsequently," Bruce said.[25]

The Bible—which charts the descendants of Abraham including Ishmael—is the foundation of faith for roughly 66% of the world's population.

Increasingly, it's being viewed as a carefully preserved tool for understanding history.

And as we've seen, it has prophesied events more dramatically than any other book known to man.

Chapter Seven

The Flipside: What Motivates Atheists?

We should start by saying that no one can make blanket statements about people as a group. But perhaps we can share insights you might agree with. They're based on numerous discussions we've had with a range of nonbelievers. Many of these folks agreed with virtually everything we're about to share.

As they told us, early on many were turned off by Christian parents, friends, or teachers, bound by rules that had little to do with the basic tenets of their faith. Many were raised in overly strict Catholic schools, with nuns rapping their knuckles every few seconds to keep them in line. I (Cord Cooper) met a former Catholic school attendee while waiting for a table at a Miami Beach restaurant. As I guessed aloud about what his childhood was like, he started to laugh, then doubled over laughing and said, "You're exactly right. And I want nothing to do with the church and religion."

This isn't a slam against Catholics, by any means. A number of Protestants are to blame for the attitudes of nonbelievers—especially those raised in restrictive homes with an endless list of "Don'ts," instead of the positives of a faith based on love and forgiveness.

A Big Tent
Others admitted they take God out of the equation to propel a sense of freedom. This is often true of those claiming vague beliefs in God but who keep repeating the mantra, "He's too busy to bother with us. It's egotistical to believe he cares about us. He doesn't." If you think about it, this flies in the face of logic. Why would God create things he cares nothing about? Yet both of these beliefs serve a useful purpose: If God doesn't exist—or exists but isn't involved in our lives— that allows us to do whatever we want. In either scenario, we become the god of our own lives.

That appealed to writer Aldous Huxley, who once admitted the reasons he was an atheist.

"I had motives for not wanting the world to have meaning; consequently assumed that it had none, and was able without any difficulty to find satisfying reasons for this assumption. . . . For myself, as no doubt, for most of my contemporaries, the philosophy of meaninglessness was essentially an instrument of liberation. The liberation we desired was simultaneous liberation from a certain political and economic system, and liberation from a certain system of morality. We objected to the morality because it interfered with our sexual freedom."

Interesting admission, isn't it? That describes a lot of people today. Perhaps yourself.

Some people are atheists or agnostics because of tragedies that happened early in life. Perhaps they lost a parent at an early age and never got over it. They ask, "How could a loving God let this happen?"

But what if the parent, through his own choices, had a terrible diet his entire life and got virtually no exercise—eating foods high in cholesterol and becoming the ultimate couch potato? How many people fit that profile?

Is that God's fault?

If the parent was killed in an auto accident, the victim of a drunk driver, was that God's fault, or the drunk driver's? You say God could have prevented the accident from happening. But wouldn't that make us puppets on a string? What else would such a God control?

We live in a world where people are able to make their own choices. We also live in a world where people make wrong choices, like the drunk driver in the example above.

Is that God's fault?

Food for Thought

I (Pat Boone) have a friend named Ken Rideout, who spent many years in Thailand, and once found himself in a debate over the existence of God with a Thai government official.

"I don't believe in any kind of God," the official said. "And if there were actually a God, one who permits all the evils that happen to innocent people, like earthquakes, famines, diseases, hurricanes, and wars, I wouldn't want to have anything to do with him anyway!"

Feeling he'd settled the argument, he waited for Ken's response. But it wasn't what he expected.

"Well, let's assume you're correct—that there is no God," Ken answered. "Don't earthquakes, hurricanes, diseases, famines, and wars exist anyway? Who do you blame them on now?"

The official cleared his throat and said, somewhat hesitantly, "Well, I guess on nature, and I guess on man himself." After a pause, Ken asked, "Then why blame these things on God? You don't rail against nature—you marvel at it."

The official had stumbled onto points outlined in Chapter Five.

Wars by definition are man-made calamities. So are events like the tragic Challenger disaster in 1986. And, as the respected relief organization, Mazon, has acknowledged on its Web site, world hunger—to a large extent—is a man-made tragedy, and highly preventable.

Through carelessness and our own human nature, we often make ourselves victims unnecessarily, as we point out in the chapter on tragedy. And as we note, natural events like hurricanes and earthquakes perform functions invaluable to planet Earth. Hurricanes help drive weather patterns and clean the oceans. Earthquakes relieve the stresses and strains between adjoining plates of the earth and at fault lines.

Chats with a Nonbeliever

My grandson Ryan is a person of faith. And just as I do, he has friends who are nonbelievers. One of them wrote me a few years ago, and he and I exchanged emails for several years on the topic of religion and the existence of God.

He says religion, particularly Christianity, is a scam, and he rejects the idea of faith.

"If we cannot comprehend God through thought," he said, "I want nothing to do with God."

Yet if God exists, he by definition is the supreme intellect of the universe—having created everything we know, and everything we don't. Even now, we understand only a small portion of the known universe, according to scientists. How could we possibly comprehend the intellect that *created* the universe? If our puny minds could readily understand God, he wouldn't be much of a God, would he?

Though he rejects the idea of faith, my grandson's friend has a definite belief system—a firm belief that God does not exist. He puts considerable *faith* in that belief system, betting that he's right, and that theists— believers in God—are wrong.

He, like other nonbelievers, feels that religion— especially Christianity—has done nothing to help humanity. Yet it can be proven that Christian principles have played a large role in the formation of our Constitution and the notion of democracy. Most of the Founding Fathers believed in Christian precepts, and the Creator is referenced in the Declaration of

Independence, correctly credited with endowing us with the "inalienable rights" that go to the root of freedom.

Ryan's friend rails against the actions of Christians, past and present, linking those actions to an "inconsistent" God. In one email, he said he'd been "horribly pained by Christian actions" against his friends. As I said in my response to him, that's a misstatement. He's undoubtedly been hurt by the actions of people who *call* themselves Christians, but certainly not by "Christian actions." If everyone actually lived Christian precepts, this world would be a different place, as Thomas Jefferson and others have said.[26]

The actions of certain people are inconsistent, because they don't live according principles they espouse. Is that God's fault, or a sign of human failure?

Like Ryan's friend, many folks see a lot of things they don't like in people who profess faith, and make the blanket decision that God doesn't exist and all religion is a sham.

They see injustices in the world, and blame a God that they don't believe exists. Anger and disillusionment are at the root of their disbelief.

Everybody has to make a choice about what to believe, and it takes faith whichever path he chooses.

1. Either a person believes in nothing, no God, no Creator, in the premise that everything we have known and depended on and enjoyed and experienced in our lives just "happened" without a plan, or

2. He believes there has been a plan, an architect who drew up a blueprint and executed it.

A lot of people have chosen option 1 because the idea of a God who is in control doesn't appeal to them, as we've noted. They don't want to bow to a supreme being or admit there are rules and guidelines, rewards and consequences. It takes faith to believe there is no God, just as it takes faith to believe there is one. But which odds would you rather take to Vegas: 50/50 odds—either that there's a God or there isn't? Or the astronomical odds against a universe like ours occurring without cause—and complex matter like DNA forming randomly, and evolving to such complexity in a relatively short period of time (see Chapter Three)?

Has Ryan's friend considered those odds?

Like others, he feels that not only is religion a crock, but so is the notion of morality. He says he's "all for having moral codes fall away. Morality should be left behind as an ancient, dull concept." Further, he says there's "no such thing as good or evil—no such thing as right or wrong"; that's part of our own construct. But think about it: If there's no such thing as right or wrong—if there is no God—there are no guidelines that matter. We can do whatever we want, and act on our own impulses. Nothing we do, whether "good" or "bad," will mean anything when we're gone—except perhaps for the terrible aftermath in the lives of those who follow. But who cares, right? All life is stupid, pointless, and temporary, many say.

While sharing their worldview, Ryan's friend and others admit to feeling empty, cynical, and lonely. And who wouldn't with this philosophy?

I have enormous respect for Ryan's buddy. He's an amazingly intelligent guy, and he and I have grown to be friends. I'm sharing nothing here that I haven't already shared with him. And to his credit, he's been receptive to what I've had to say, apparently without changing his mind.

But let's look again at a couple of his statements: "Morality should be left behind as an ancient, dull concept. There's no such thing as good or evil—no such thing as right or wrong." If that's true, what if someone brutally murdered a person close to him? Would he demand the murderer be punished? Probably so. But why, if there's no such thing as good or evil? The killer was simply acting on his own instincts, doing what he felt like at the time. If there's no such thing as right or wrong, why should he be punished?

He says, "Belief is what creates 'evil.'" Yet he has his own belief system—a belief in nothingness, a belief that God doesn't exist.

Does that belief *also* create (or enable) evil?

I've asked a lot of the same questions he has. I've pursued a lot of the same thought, and been willing to accept the nonexistence of God if that were true. But I've discovered that not to be the case. I've found a rewarding path of faith that's given me a power greater than myself.

Yes, many religious people are hypocrites, and yes, lots of people believe some goofy things and hate others who don't agree. And yes, many terrible things have been done in the name of religion and Christianity. But that doesn't discredit God or his love. It simply points up how stupid and willful and hateful people can be when they disregard his precepts.

As I said, Ryan's bud and I have become good friends—so much so that, when he was considering marriage, he asked me to be a "co-officiator" at his wedding. He asked me to act under the authority of the officiating minister (the latter chosen either out of tradition or at the request of his fiancée). The point is, even though we disagreed on spiritual issues, he wanted me to be with him on the most important day of his life. He saw me as a trusted friend, and still does. The reason? We were able to have frank and open discussions without anger or without my preaching to him. We became closer as a result.

Wouldn't it be great if we could all do that?

Questionable PR

We've talked a lot in this chapter about people who are poor representatives of their cause. Let's sketch out a quick scenario to wrap up the point.

Say an author has a new book published, filled with amazing facts and discoveries. He also includes some statements that are controversial, but rooted in the best interests of his readers. Two PR agents contact him to tout the book.

One turns out to be inept, taking the author's statements out of context without fully reading—or knowing the meaning of—the book. Before he knows it, the author is bombarded with hate mail from people who've heard the misstatements.

The other agent reads the book and presents an accurate picture. The book gets mixed results. Many buy it, based on the accurate portrayal, and readers' lives are changed.

But because of publicity from the "idiot agent," many buy the book, read passages out of context, and throw it in the trash. Others read the entire book, but with a preconceived bias—an agenda driven by what the agent ineptly publicized. They read the book through their own filter, seeing what they want to see. They declare the author "dead to them" and put him out of their minds. To them, he effectively doesn't exist.

As far as the facts are concerned, who's at fault for the miscommunication—the author, or the inept agent? If you think about it, that agent is like many so-called Christians—who claim to represent a faith whose tenets they don't follow, misquoting a book they've misinterpreted or seldom read.

Many of these people don't stop there; they hurt others through actions totally inconsistent with the faith they espouse.

Is that God's fault—or the result of fallible humans going their own way, without consulting (or correctly understanding) the source they claim to represent?

Rays on the Beach

Earlier we talked about one of the appeals of atheism, of being the god of your own existence. I (co-author Cord Cooper) had a great chat with a surfer on South Beach who explained himself a lot more plainly than Aldous Huxley, mentioned earlier. As we spoke, the guy said straight out: "Yeah, I'm the god of my own existence, man, and I'm having a blast!" We laughed and knuckled each other on his honesty. But then I asked this question: "What happens when you discover that you alone aren't enough to get through a tragedy or insurmountable loss?" He looked at me, surprised by the question, then stared at the ocean.

"I dunno, man. I'll figure it out when I get there."

We both sat silent.

He got up, said, "Nice meetin' ya, bro," and walked off.

Life can be great, and life can present challenges. It can be pretty scary meeting them alone.

Does that make God a crutch? A talk-show host asked minister Greg Laurie that question. Said Laurie: "He's not a crutch. He's the whole hospital."

The host—a well-known agnostic—looked down for a few seconds. He looked up at Laurie and shot back, "Good answer."

As we said, life can be cool, and life can be rough. And we're all on a journey.

We hope you'll read the next chapter with the same tool that got you this far. An open mind.

We ask some tough questions, and the answers may surprise you.

Chapter Eight

Was Jesus the Son of God?

Jesus claimed to be God—the second person of the Trinity, God's son. Was he who he said he was? Or was he the biggest liar who ever lived? Was he misquoted by his followers? And for that matter, did he even exist? To look at these questions, we need to ask a few more.

Among them:

Weren't the Gospels written in the second century, long after Jesus' apostles had died?
Though it was once fashionable to date the book of Acts and other New Testament documents to between the early and mid-second century, most scholars now

date these writings closer to Jesus' lifetime. Many date the Gospels to the 70s-90s A.D. A number of others date Acts and three of the Gospels to the 60s—narrowing the date of some of the books to the early 60s—well within the lifespan of eyewitnesses to Jesus' ministry, says Craig Blomberg, Ph.D., a noted scholar. A key component scholars look at when dating the Gospels is the internal evidence, a close examination of the writings themselves.

To date the Gospels, Blomberg says, you need to look first at the book of Acts, which covered the events of the early church and was written by Luke as a sequel to his Gospel. According to scholars including Blomberg, Acts contains internal evidence that has helped lead to an earlier dating of the Gospels. "The abrupt end of [Acts], with the apostle Paul awaiting the results of his appeal to Caesar in Rome, has suggested to many that Luke wrote almost immediately after these last events occurred," Blomberg said.[27]

Luke spends eight chapters (Acts 21-28)—more than a quarter of the book—detailing "Paul's arrest, his various hearings, and his imprisonments," all building toward Paul's appeal to Caesar, Blomberg noted. To many scholars, it makes little sense that Luke wouldn't have recorded the outcome of that appeal "if he had written at a late enough date to have known it," he said.

The appeal resulted in Paul's freedom. That's a detail Luke surely would have included had it occurred before he finished writing Acts.

A key to dating the book is Paul's two-year house arrest in Rome, prior to the outcome of the appeal. That period is pegged to 60-62, Blomberg said, "since Festus [a Roman governor] acceded to power in 59 and Paul was shipped to Rome" shortly thereafter.[28]

Luke carefully recorded all pertinent facts, so the omission of Paul's release—circa 62—is critical. Many scholars thus date Acts to the early 60s, while Paul was still under house arrest, with a number of them pegging the date to 62 A.D.

As mentioned, Acts is a sequel to the Gospel According to Luke. "This would require a date for Luke's Gospel . . . no later than about A.D. 62," Blomberg noted.[29]

Most scholars believe Mark's Gospel was the earliest of the four, and Blomberg and others say it was likely written a year or two before Luke's.

Blomberg and a number of other scholars date Matthew's Gospel to pre-70 A.D. A key factor again is the internal evidence. Why would Matthew "include references to the temple tax (17:24–27), offerings (5:23–24) and ritual (23:16–22) . . . in an era (after 70) in which none of these was practiced any longer?" Blomberg said. "Why would he stress Jesus' antagonism against the Sadducees in an age in which they had died out?" The Gospel writers displayed a "consistent pattern of selecting episodes from Jesus' life that were theologically meaningful for their communities," he said.[30] Emphasizing outdated references and practices would not fit that pattern.

A number of scholars date John's Gospel to the 80s or 90s, likely "during the reign of Domitian (81–96), when John was a very old man ministering in Ephesus," said Blomberg. According to records from antiquity, witnesses recorded that John was indeed long-lived, strengthening the case for his authorship of the Gospel during this later period.

Do any non-biblical sources mention Jesus or corroborate events in the Gospels?

According to scholars, there are roughly a dozen non-biblical references to Jesus and other figures mentioned in the Gospels. One of the more notable is from first-century historian Josephus. Below is a passage from his work, *The Antiquities*:

"At this time there appeared Jesus, a wise man, for he was a doer of startling deeds, a teacher of people who received the truth with pleasure. He gained a following both among many Jews and among many of Greek origin. And when Pilate, because of accusations made by the leading man among us, condemned him to the cross, those who had loved him previously did not cease to do so. And up until this very day the tribe of Christians, named after him, has not died out."

Josephus was a Jew who didn't convert to Christianity. That makes some of the statements in this passage all the more remarkable.

The Antiquities traces the history of Jews from the dawn of recorded time through the late first century.

In it, Josephus tells how a high priest named Ananias took advantage of the death of the Roman governor Festus—who is also mentioned in the New Testament—in order to have James, the brother of Jesus, killed.

Josephus writes:

"[Ananias] convened a meeting of the Sanhedrin and brought before them a man named James, the brother of Jesus, who was called the Christ, and certain others. He accused them of having transgressed the law and delivered them up to be stoned."

A number of other sources reference events not only in the Gospels but the book of Acts.

Did Matthew, Mark, Luke, and John really write the Gospels attributed to them?

Matthew was a former tax collector. In that culture and subsequent ones, tax collectors weren't simply disliked; they were reviled. If Christians later falsely attributed authorship, they wouldn't have picked a tax collector, many scholars agree. They'd have chosen someone with gravitas to bolster the Gospel's credibility.

As for Luke, he was "a relatively obscure figure," said Blomberg. "He as not among the best-known of Paul's companions, nor was he an apostle himself, so it seems unlikely that anyone would have fictitiously attributed a Gospel to him."[31]

Some critics have disputed the authorship of Mark's Gospel, but their reasons don't hold up, Blomberg says. Some say "the author could not have been Mark, the companion of the apostle Paul, because the Gospel shows no contact with Pauline theology." That reasoning is flawed, says Blomberg. "An emphasis on the cross [as reflected in Mark] is in fact one of Paul's theological centerpieces."[32]

Given that Mark was not one of the disciples and was a relatively unknown figure, it's unlikely "anyone unfamiliar with the author of this Gospel but desiring to credit it to an authoritative witness would have selected Mark as his man," Blomberg said.[33]

In addition, there's a telling note about the Gospel of John. Aside from being listed as author, the apostle John "never appears by name in the Gospel, while the John that does appear is always the Baptist, without ever being called by that title. Unless John the apostle were known to be the author of this document, surely the omission of further clarification as to which 'John' was in view would be surprising," Blomberg said.[34]

Some critics nevertheless question the authorship of John's Gospel. One reason? They claim John was illiterate, based on Acts 4:13.

Said Blomberg: "The view that John was illiterate is based on a mistranslation of Acts 4:13, which affirms only that John did not have formal rabbinic training."[35] This is also the view of noted Greek scholars including T.J. McCrossan.

For further reading, Blomberg offers this: "The detailed evidence for [sequentially] narrowing down the author of this Gospel to [a person of Jewish heritage], from Israel, an eyewitness, an apostle, and then John is classically stated by B. F. Westcott, author of *The Gospel According to St. John*."

What about critics' assertions that Jesus never claimed to be divine?

Some skeptics have said the Gospel of John's

assertions about Jesus' divinity are incompatible with the synoptic Gospels (Matthew, Mark, and Luke), and that only John's Gospel focuses on Jesus' divinity. Not so, say McCrossan, Blomberg and other scholars. The divinity issue is underscored throughout the Gospels. "In the synoptics you get a whole rash of phenomena, including the passage where Peter and others in the boat worship Jesus (Matthew 14) at the end of his walking on the water," Blomberg said in a telephone interview.

"Following Peter's confession of Jesus as the Christ on the road to Caesarea Philippi (Mark 8:27–30), Jesus begins teaching about his coming suffering and death," said Blomberg.[36]

In addition, the term "Son of God" occurs at "strategic places in Mark's Gospel to highlight Jesus' exalted role," he said. "'Son of God' forms part of Mark's 'headline' to the Gospel (1:1) and recurs again as part of the Roman centurion's climactic confession at the time of Jesus' death (15:39).

"The other title Mark introduces in his opening verse is 'Christ' (the Greek equivalent to the Hebrew, 'Messiah'). This title . . . does not recur until Peter's dramatic confession in 8:29 (and then six times thereafter). But all of chapters 1–8 . . . build toward that confession," said Blomberg.[37]

In addition, Luke and Matthew describe Christ's virginal conception. All of this hardly makes John's Gospel unique, scholars say.

Did the Gospel authors think they were writing history?

"Gospel" means "good news." The key word in that phrase is "news" When a person shares good news, he's sharing facts. Otherwise, why bother? Yet skeptics claim that the Gospel writers were not recording facts or preserving history. The question is, why would they do otherwise, spreading a story they knew deep down wasn't true?

Ten of the eleven remaining disciples endured violent deaths for spreading the good news of Jesus. Among them: Matthew. Peter was hanged on a cross upside down. Apostles including Stephen were also killed. Why would they and others willingly die for a work of fiction?

Is there other evidence Jesus was who he said he was?

Take, for example, Paul. Formerly known as Saul of Tarsus, he had been a Pharisee who viewed Christians as heretics and persecuted them with a vengeance.

But his life took a dramatic turn on the road to

Damascus, where he witnessed the resurrected Christ. It was Jesus' appearance that impelled Paul to become a dominant proclaimer of the Gospel.

In the natural, Paul had nothing to gain—not financially, not in stature, not in any way—by joining followers of Christ. He knew that his conversion meant humiliation and near-certain death. Why would he face such a fate if he hadn't seen something truly amazing on that Damascus road?

Another example: James, the brother of Jesus. He'd been a doubter during most of Christ's ministry, but Jesus appeared to him after the Resurrection. The result: A life-changing experience much like Paul's. James went on to become a leader in the Christian church.

If he was going to support his brother's ministry, wouldn't it have made more sense when Christ was drawing huge crowds and performing miracles prior to the crucifixion?

According to Harvard University evidence expert Simon Greenleaf, something amazing must have happened after Jesus' death for James to have done such a dramatic 180.

Yet another example: The 500 to whom Jesus appeared—also after the Resurrection. There's no record of anyone denying this happened. No denials by

Josephus or other first-century historians. Not one of the 500 later denied the appearance had occurred.

What about contradictions in the Gospels?

In the first three Gospels Jesus refers to himself as the "Son of man." Critics have claimed this shows Jesus referring to his humanity, not his divinity. But is this an example of contradiction, or consistency?

"Son of man" is not a reference to Jesus' humanity. It's a reference to Daniel 7:13-14 in the Old Testament, scholars say.

Here are the words from the prophet Daniel:

"In my vision at night I looked, and there before me was one like a Son of man, coming with the clouds of heaven. He approached the Ancient of days and was led into his presence. He was given authority, glory, and sovereign power; all peoples, nations and men of every language worshiped him. His dominion is an everlasting dominion that will not pass away, and his kingdom is one that will never by destroyed."

In using the phrase "Son of man," Daniel is describing the Messiah. When Jesus describes himself using this term, he underscores his divinity.

In virtually every case, say scholars, so-called inconsistencies can be explained.

In a story recounting one of Jesus' healings, Matthew says a centurion asked Jesus to heal his servant. Luke says the centurion sent elders to ask for the healing. Both accounts are consistent, Blomberg says. In antiquity, "when one sent an emissary, it was as though he himself had spoken. That's true even now," he noted. "Reporters all the time will say, 'The president today announced such and such,' and then you see the video clip and you find it's the press secretary who's speaking. The president did speak, but through his press secretary."

Bottom line: The centurion made the request and asked the elders to deliver the message. Matthew and Mark both record that the centurion asked for the healing.

According to a range of scholars, the Gospels are amazingly consistent, considering they were written by four different people at different locations.

Said Greenleaf of Harvard Law School: "There is enough of a [variation] to show that there could have been no previous concert among them; and at the same time such substantial agreement as to show that they all were independent narrators of the same great transaction."

Do Jesus' teachings reflect a calling from a higher power?

In his Gospel, John quotes Christ in the 13th chapter,

35th verse: "By this shall all men know that ye are my disciples, if ye have love one for another." In other words, love is the hallmark of all true followers of Christ.

If a person needs your shirt, Jesus says you should also give him your coat. Over and over through the New Testament he tells his followers to love and be tolerant. To turn the other cheek. To not be vengeful or quick to anger. To "judge not lest ye be judged."

Jesus' teachings are based in part on the Ten Commandments, but he takes those tenets a whole lot further.

According to many biblical scholars, not only do Jesus' teachings set him apart, they define the chasm between God and man—the difference between what we are called to be, and the sorry state in which we find ourselves.

Doubt it? Consider this: If everyone—individually and as nations—lived the teachings of Jesus every second of every day without letup, we'd need no locks on doors, no bars on windows. We'd need no spy satellites, no Interpol. No police officers or jails. No FBI. No CIA. No armed forces (there'd be no wars or the need for national defense). Lawyers and judges would be superfluous because people would peacefully settle their differences.

We'd live in a perfect world. There'd have been no Holocaust. No Nazi regime. No Pol-Pot horrors in Cambodia. No suicide bombings in Israel. No 9/11 or al-Qaida.

Instead of turning jets into missiles, Osama bin Laden would've turned millions of dollars into food for the hungry. Instead of slaughtering his own people, Saddam Hussein would have allowed them to forge their own destinies.

Sound ridiculous? That's because we're so used to the world the way it is versus the way Christ called it to be.

Reread the last four paragraphs above, then answer this question. Is there any doubt this world would be transformed, becoming heaven on Earth, if everyone— everybody, all the time—followed to the letter the Ten Commandments and the teachings of Christ? Never killing or stealing. Never lying. Judging not. Feeding the hungry. Clothing the poor.

If you're saying at this point, "Sounds like a pretty boring world," ask yourself whether Holocaust survivors would consider that a boring world. Whether relatives of 9/11 victims would consider it a boring world. Whether families of the millions slaughtered by Stalin—or the dead in all the wars ever fought—would consider it a boring world.

135

The New Testament takes God's interaction with man to a higher level. God replicates himself in human form and offers himself in love for all mankind. Through grace, we're called to a higher purpose.

The vast difference between what we are and what we're called to be stands as evidence of our fallen nature. And if you doubt that fallen nature, look no further than the crucifixion. Christ came in peace, yet how did we treat him?

Did any of Jesus' contemporaries deny the impact of his miracles?

Though members of the Sanhedrin turned Jesus over to Pilate, they couldn't deny his power. Nor could anyone else. Not the historian Josephus, as noted earlier, nor the eyewitnesses of his ministry. Doubters later called Christ a sorcerer—"which acknowledges the fact that he performed amazing deeds," Blomberg notes—but no one ever denied his power as recorded in the Gospels.

Consider this: Jerusalem spanned a relatively small area in which distorted or false claims about Jesus would have quickly become common knowledge, McCrossan notes. Somebody would have come forward to deny the Gospels' accuracy if they had contained lies or exaggerations.

Instead, the Christian movement took hold swiftly and dramatically in Jerusalem and beyond.

Did Jesus intend to start a new religion?

Christ came to trade the laws of religion for the grace and love of a relationship with God. The word "Christian" was not used by the early church—it was a name given to believers by their enemies, according to Peter Gammons and other biblical scholars. Early believers called themselves "followers of the way." "They did not see themselves as 'converts to Christianity,' which is a Gentile concept, but complete or fulfilled Jews," Gammons said.[38]

Read the apostle Paul's words: "I say then, Hath God cast away his people? God forbid. For I also am an Israelite, of the seed of Abraham, of the tribe of Benjamin" (Romans 11:1). As Gammons points out, Paul didn't say "I *was* an Israelite."

"It is a misconception that one cannot be both Jewish and a believer in Yeshua," Gammons said. Jesus came for everyone, people of all backgrounds and traditions.

Do Old Testament prophecies support the Gospel accounts of Jesus?

Read the prophecies below and judge for yourself. Straight out of the Old Testament, these prophecies clearly foretell a coming Messiah. The descriptions of Jesus—written hundreds of years before he was born—are compelling, a number of scholars note.

Old Testament prophecy: "For unto us a child is born, unto us a son is given: and the government shall be upon his shoulder: and his name shall be called Wonderful, Counselor, the mighty God, the everlasting Father, the Prince of Peace" (Isaiah 9:6).

"Many unbelievers have charged Christianity with changing the Old Testament vision of the Messiah," said the late scholar D. James Kennedy, who held nine degrees and headed one of the nation's largest Presbyterian churches. "[Doubters] claim that the Old Testament speaks only of a national deliverer who would be an extraordinary man, and yet just a man and not God. However, a careful study of the titles that Isaiah uses in this prophecy declares that the coming Messiah would be God in the flesh."[39]

In addition to the divine attributes "Wonderful" and "Counselor," which is how the prophet describes Yahweh in Isaiah 28:29, the indisputable phrase "the mighty God" is included. "This same term is used again in Isaiah 10:21, referring to God," Kennedy said. And there is this intriguing reference: ". . .the government shall be upon his shoulder. . . ." As even skeptics have grudgingly conceded, many of Jesus' teachings have formed the basis of Western law. Jesus taught tolerance, acceptance, and freedom—Christian principles that have become embedded in Western civilization. The impact of Jesus has only grown greater with time.

The prophecy above was written seven hundred years before Christ was born.

Old Testament prophecy: "But thou, Bethlehem Ephratah, though thou be little among the thousands of Judah, yet out of thee shall he come forth unto me that is to be ruler in Israel; whose goings forth have been from of old, from everlasting" (Micah 5:2).

Hundreds of years before the fact, the prophet Micah declared Jesus would be born in the small town of Bethlehem, also known as the city of David. This "ruler in Israel" came not to rule with force but to rule men's hearts, biblical scholar T.J. McCrossan explains.

Note the phrase, "whose goings forth have been from old, *from everlasting*." This is a reference to the eternal God, replicated in human form in the person of Christ, McCrossan notes. John 8:42 confirms this prophecy: "I proceeded forth and came from God."

Micah's prophecy was written in the eighth century B.C.

Old Testament prophecy: "Therefore the Lord himself shall give you a sign; Behold, a virgin shall conceive, and bear a son. . . ." (Isaiah 7:14.)

In the New Testament, Luke 1:26-35 records this prophecy's fulfillment.

Old Testament prophecy: "But he was wounded for our transgressions, he was bruised for our iniquities: the chastisement of our peace was upon him; and with his stripes we are healed. . . . He was oppressed, and he was afflicted, yet he opened not his mouth: he is brought as a lamb to the slaughter, and as a sheep before her shearers is dumb, so he openeth not his mouth. . . .And he made his grave with the wicked, and with the rich in his death; because he had done no violence, neither was any deceit in his mouth. . . . Therefore will I divide him a portion with the great, and he shall divide the spoil with the strong; because he hath poured out his soul unto death: and he was numbered with the transgressors; and he bore the sin of many, and made intercession for the transgressors" (Isaiah 53:5, 7, 9, 12).

This passage isn't a contradiction to the prophecy declaring "his name shall be called Wonderful, Counselor, the mighty God. . . ." During his time on Earth, Jesus was both hailed and reviled.

The passage in Isaiah 53 foretells the suffering of Christ and the atoning work accomplished by his death.

The prophecy's fulfillment is outlined in the Gospels. "For even the Son of man came not to be ministered unto, but to minister, and to give his life a ransom for many. . . . And Pilate asked him again, saying, Answerest thou nothing? Behold how many things they witness against thee. But Jesus yet answered nothing, so that Pilate marveled. . . . And with him they crucified two thieves; the one on his right hand, and the other on his left. And the scripture was fulfilled, which saith, And he was numbered with the transgressors" (Mark 10:45; 15:4-5, 27-28).

"When the even was come, there came a rich man of Arimathaea, named Joseph, who also himself was Jesus' disciple. . . . And laid it [Christ's body] in his own new tomb, which he had hewn out in the rock: and he rolled a great stone to the door of the sepulcher, and departed" (Matthew 27:57, 60).

"Isaiah points out that the Christ would not attempt to defend himself before his accusers, but would voluntarily give his life as a sacrifice," Kennedy noted.

"Isaiah also foretold that the Messiah 'made his grave with the wicked, but with the rich in his death.' This was fulfilled when Jesus was crucified with common criminals and then placed in a rich man's tomb."[40]

Old Testament prophecy: "Rejoice greatly, O my people. Shout with joy. For look—your King is coming. He is the Righteous One, the Victor. Yet he is lowly, riding on a donkey's colt" (Zechariah 9:9; LB).

In the New Testament, Mark describes the scene: "So the colt was brought to Jesus and the disciples threw their cloaks across its back for him to ride on. Then many in the crowd spread out their coats along the road before him, while others threw down leafy branches from the fields. He was in the center of the procession with crowds ahead and behind. . . . And so he entered Jerusalem and went into the temple" (Mark 11:7-9, 11; Living Bible).

Hundreds of years before Christ was born, the Old Testament predicted the Messiah would be hailed riding the foal of a donkey, signifying he would come not in military might but in the spirit of humility and peace, T.J. McCrossan explains.

Old Testament prophecy: "The voice of him that crieth in the wilderness, Prepare ye the way of the Lord, make straight in the desert a highway for our God. Every valley shall be exalted and every mountain and hill shall be made low: and the crooked shall be made straight, and the rough place plain: And the glory of the Lord shall be revealed, and all flesh shall see it together: for the mouth of the Lord hath spoken it"

(Isaiah 40:3-5).

This prophecy predicts a special messenger "would come in the power and spirit of Elijah the prophet. He would turn the hearts of Israel back to God and prepare them to recognize the Messiah," Kennedy said. "These prophecies were fulfilled by John the Baptist [Matthew 11:13-14]. He came as a prophet to proclaim God's Word and call the nation of Israel to repentance. As a Nazarite, he was set apart by God as a special witness [Luke 1:15]."[41]

The New Testament Gospel writer, Luke, couldn't be clearer about the fulfillment of this prophecy:

"The word of God came unto John, the son of Zacharias, in the wilderness. And he came into all the country about Jordan, preaching the baptism of repentance for the remission of sins; As it is written in the book of the words of Esaias [Isaiah] the prophet, saying, The voice of one crying in the wilderness, Prepare ye the way of the Lord, make his paths straight" (Luke 3:2-4).

What about the claim that Jesus didn't really die on the cross but swooned, or fainted?

(The following by definition covers unpleasant details. If they get to be too graphic, feel free to skip to page 149: "Did the Resurrection occur?")

There was no way Jesus could have survived a Roman crucifixion, according to Alex Metherell, a noted physician, engineer and research scientist who has been a consultant to the National Institutes of Health at Bethesda, Maryland, and is a former University of California professor.

"The executions typically started with a flogging, which was so severe that many victims died before they got up to the crucifixion site," he said.

"The whips used by the Romans were like a cat-of-nine-tails, with pieces of heavy metal and sharp shards of bone tied into the leather thongs. When they struck the back, the sharp, knife-like edges of the bone dug into the flesh and the heavy metal caused severe bruising. When the Roman yanked the whip away, the bone shards tore the flesh. So Christ was lacerated from the top of his back to his legs.

"There were often two Romans doing the flogging, one on each side of the prisoner. Each soldier alternately whipped Christ across his shoulders, back, buttocks, and legs. Each blow of the whip was like the claws of a lion ripping the flesh."

Given the construction of the whips and the severity of the beating, Christ likely would have been in even worse shape than that portrayed in the film *The Passion of the Christ*, Metherell said in a phone interview from his Southern California home.

"The blood lost as a result of the scourging would have put Christ into hypovolemic (low blood volume) shock. In this state he would have difficulty standing upright and would tend to pass out. This is consistent with his difficulty carrying the horizontal cross beam to the execution site."

The vertical beam was planted in the ground at the site. "When he got there, he would be in critical condition. Hypovolemic shock results in a low return of blood to the heart due to volume loss. This causes a severe drop in blood pressure. To compensate, the heart beats harder and faster, a condition called tachycardia.

"The hypovolemic shock would have worsened with the journey up the hill to the site. As the heart is failing under the stress—a typical result of hypovolemic shock—a pericardial effusion of clear straw-colored fluid begins to collect between the outside of the heart and the pericardial sac." Metherell explained.

"Christ's breathing would also increase, likely resulting in a pleural effusion of similar fluid in the pleural space between the outside of the lungs and the pleura inside the rib cage."

With his body in severe trauma, Christ was forced on the ground at the execution site and nailed to the horizontal beam, with his arms outstretched in a straight line.

"The nailing was done through the wrists because it was the only effective anchor point," he said. "That means the nails would slash through the carpal tunnel and crush the median nerve, the biggest nerve in the arm. The pain from that alone would be indescribable. When he was lifted up to be placed on the vertical beam, he was dangling from the cross beam, supported only by those two nails.

"As soon as he was lifted up off the ground, gravity would abruptly force his body downward and his arms and shoulders would immediately be dislocated. When the dislocation stretched his arms by about four inches, his arms would be hanging at a 30- to 40-degree angle. This would produce huge tension on his chest.

"As his arms were being dislocated and stretched, the wrists were rotating on the nails, which meant the nails were grinding on the crushed median nerve. The Romans then attached him to the vertical beam, and affixed his legs to the post. They placed his feet so that he was in a half knee-bend position and drove a nail transversely through the heel bones, confirmed through the archaeological discoveries of other crucifixion victims."

The fact Jesus was in a half knee-bend position

eliminated any form of support he might get from the nails in his feet, Metherell said. "Even a healthy person can't maintain his weight in a half knee-bend position for long, so he remained in a hanging position, with his body weight supported by the arms." This meant his chest was pulled to an inhaled position. "When you inhale, your ribs rotate up as your chest inflates. The diaphragm contracts and flattens. The inhaled position obviously makes it extremely difficult to breathe. The process of dying by crucifixion is primarily that of slow suffocation.

"Not being able to breathe properly would result in a condition called respiratory acidosis. The latter increases the impulse to breathe, making the torture worse. To breathe, he had to push up on his heels, and as he went up, the angle of the arms changed slightly, with the nails grinding through the crushed median nerve. As he pushed up, his back—filled with open wounds from the flogging—would be rubbing against the rough vertical beam, reopening lacerations that were primarily horizontal. That would cause more bleeding.

"Eventually, what little strength he had gave out. Since he could no longer push up on his legs to breathe, his breathing became very shallow, increasing the respiratory acidosis. All of this caused a rapid heart rate and a barely detectable pulse. The pericardial and pleural effusions sent fluid into the space around the heart and lungs. He experienced cardiac arrhythmia, cardiac arrest, and his heart stopped beating.

"To confirm that Jesus was dead, a soldier took his spear and thrust it into his side. [Based on the Gospel accounts] the spear probably went in through the right frontal part of the chest, penetrating the chest wall, then went through the pleural space of the right lung, the pericardial space and into the right ventricle of the heart.

"The pleural and pericardial spaces contained the clear, slightly straw-colored fluid that looks like water. When the spear was withdrawn, the clear water fluid would come out first, followed by the blood from the right ventricle. The description in the New Testament, of blood and water flowing out, is medically accurate."

In the interview with Metherell, he cited an article in the *Journal of the American Medical Association*, which said, "Clearly, the weight of the historical and medical evidence indicates that Jesus was dead before the wound to his side was inflicted. . . . Accordingly, interpretations based on the assumption that Jesus did not die on the cross [are] at odds with modern medical knowledge."

What about passages in the Gospels indicating the Romans drove nails through Jesus' hands?

There's no contradiction, say scholars. Words in New Testament Greek and Hebrew often have a wider semantic connotation than English. What was translated in English as hand actually meant *hand and arm* (including of course the wrist) in New Testament Greek.

Did the Resurrection occur?

Think about the answers to these questions: Did Jesus die on the cross? We've already described in detail how Jesus could not have survived the crucifixion. Did he appear to people sometime later? We have eyewitness accounts in the four Gospels, as well as non-biblical references by the historian Josephus, about excitement building among early Christians after the crucifixion.

It was Josephus who wrote that Jesus' brother James—a post-Resurrection convert who became leader of the Jerusalem church—suffered a violent death for his beliefs. This non-biblical reference by a respected early historian is significant. Why? It offers additional corroboration that Jesus' followers were willing to die for the One they saw resurrected.

Then there are the other apostles. "In forty days, these men who were afraid to suffer with their leader were transformed into bold and fearless witnesses," D. James Kennedy said. "Most of the apostles were eventually condemned to a martyr's death. To believe that the apostles would suffer persecution and death for what they knew to be a lie is beyond credible belief."[42]

Finally, there is the most famous of the apostles—Paul—whom most scholars agree wrote 1 Corinthians. It was Paul's face-to-face encounter with the risen Christ on the road to Damascus that led to his conversion. As we've said, he was formerly known as Saul of Tarsus, a Pharisee who hated and persecuted Christians. What did he have to gain by converting and leaving the Jewish faith? He knew his conversion would lead to certain death—and he wound up paying for his faith with the ultimate sacrifice. Why would he willingly die if he hadn't witnessed the resurrected Jesus?

In Corinthians Paul admits being an eyewitness to the risen Christ. "Am I not an apostle? . . . Have I not seen Jesus Christ our Lord?" he writes in 1 Corinthians 9:1. In 1 Corinthians 15:5-8, Paul says this: "[After the Resurrection, Jesus] appeared to Peter, and then to the twelve [disciples]. After that, he appeared to more than 500 of the brothers at the same time, most of whom are still living, though some have fallen asleep. Then he appeared to James, then to all the apostles. And last of all he appeared to me also."

And so we ask the question again: Why would a Jew convert to a heretical sect—one he himself had condemned—if he hadn't indeed seen something life-changing? Why would he so openly admit to seeing Jesus if he hadn't?

There are other interesting points in the Corinthians passage: The reference to 500 eyewitnesses, most of whom "are still living."

The non-biblical literature of the time shows not one contradiction regarding the claims of Paul or other eyewitnesses of Christ's Resurrection.

Christ's appearances after the crucifixion are referenced throughout the Gospels and Acts.

Examples: He appeared to Mary Magdalene (John 20: 11-18), to the disciples after appearing to Mary (John 20: 19-23; Matthew 28:10) to the disciples again, this time including Thomas (John 20: 24-30; Matthew 28: 16-20), on the road to Emmaus (Luke 24: 13-32), and to the apostles at the Mount of Olives prior to his ascension (Acts 1: 4-9 and Luke 24: 50-52).

Lee Strobel, former legal affairs reporter for the *Chicago Tribune*—who covered dozens of trials both civil and criminal—says this about the number of eyewitnesses who saw Christ after the Resurrection, including the disciples and the 500 mentioned by Paul:

"If you were to call each one of the witnesses to a court of law to be cross-examined for just 15 minutes each, and you went around the clock without a break, it would take . . . 129 straight hours of eyewitness testimony. Who could possibly walk away unconvinced?"[43]

Simon Greenleaf—the famed lawyer and Harvard professor who wrote the widely hailed *Treatise on the Law of Evidence*—once said that if any unbiased jury was presented with the evidence for the Resurrection, they would conclude it to be a historical fact.

To put things in perspective, consider this from J.P. Moreland, who earned a degree in chemistry from the University of Missouri and a Ph.D in philosophy from USC. He gives this brief overview of Christ's time on Earth, starting before the crucifixion:

"A rabbi named Jesus appears from a lower-class region. He teaches for three years, gathers a following of lower- and middle-class people, gets in trouble with the authorities, and gets crucified along with 30,000 other Jewish men who are executed during this time period.

"But five weeks after he's crucified, over 10,000 Jews [have had life-changing experiences attributable to his ministry]. And get this: They're willing to give up or alter all five of the social institutions that they've been taught since childhood."44

Moreland's conclusion? This was no ordinary man. Something remarkable happened after his death. The Resurrection caused a chain reaction of events that spread Christianity through the Roman Empire and eventually through the world. And 2,000 years later, people are still being changed by the power and forgiving love of Christ. Why? Because his love transcends anything we could ever know. His peace passes human understanding. His hope is eternal.

Christ was God come to Earth—not to rule the world, but to renew the human mind.

He didn't come to judge; he came to uplift. He didn't come to shine a light on human weakness; he came to impart strength.

He witnessed the frustration of short-term happiness; he offered eternal joy. He witnessed the familiarity of despair and disappointment—he came to fill our emptiness with purpose and hope.

Emptiness is one of the most common feelings humans face. No amount of money can fill it. No amount of booze, sex, or drugs can numb the pain. It's a void that only God's welcoming, unconditional love can fill.

Without it, every road eventually leads to a "Then what?" You may not yet have reached that point, but sooner or later you will. You could be CEO of the world's biggest corporation. The richest person in your industry. Top gun of your profession. And there's still something missing. So you set a new goal. You figure, "If I accomplish X, Y, and Z, I'll be happy. I'll be fulfilled." You reach those goals and you're still running on empty.

Something's still missing. You don't feel complete.

Then what?

A sense that life is meaningless. To blur it, you stay busy 24/7. Stay busy long enough and you won't have time to think about it. If booze is your crutch, you try another round of that.

But no matter what, reality creeps in. And nothing changes.

If you haven't yet reached that empty place, consider this. Many of us are just one event away from complete hopelessness. You may think you have it made. But what if the one thing that means the world to you were suddenly gone? It could be your spouse. Your children. Your bank account. Think for a moment. What if that irreplaceable part of your life suddenly vanished? We live in a world where almost anything's possible.

Christ's gift of love can fill the void no matter what happens. His gift is eternal. Unchangeable. But for a gift—any gift—to be yours, you have to accept it. Picture a spectacularly wrapped package placed in the middle of a table. The card on it says it's yours alone. Until you accept it—until you take possession of it—it's not yours.

Christ is the ultimate gift of love. Why not accept that gift, even amid your doubts? He came to make the unknown known. To make the darkness light. Why not say right now, "God, if you're out there, accept me as I am. I give you my past, my present, my future. Come into my life. Forgive me for all the times I've missed the mark. Fill me with your presence. Fill me with a love that will not let me go. I welcome you as both partner and friend. I welcome Christ as Savior and Lord. Guide me day by day. Cause me to trust you moment by moment, until that day when I see you face to face. Thank you, God. Thank you. Amen."

If you prayed that prayer and meant it, you've just begun a journey. The most amazing journey you will ever take.

If you didn't pray the prayer but simply read the words, don't escape Christ's love. Those words are now part of you. Make them a prayer, and let the evidence of God change you forever.

Notes

Chapter One:
1: This is the rotation speed at the equator. The planet's rotation speed varies by location.

Chapter Two:
2: Brian Greene, *The Fabric of the Cosmos* (New York, N.Y.: Knopf Publishing Group, 2005).
3: *ibid.*

Chapter Three:
4: Paul Davies, *The Cosmic Blueprint* (New York: Simon and Schuster, 1988).
5: William Lane Craig, "A Response to Grünbaum on Creation and Big Bang Cosmology." Philosophia Naturalis, 31 (1994): 237-249.
6: *ibid.*
7: *ibid.*
8: Victor Stenger, based on a chapter from *The Unconscious Quantum* (Amherst, N.Y.: Prometheus Books, 1995).

Chapter Four:

9: Dale Matthews, *The Faith Factor: Proof of the Healing Power of Prayer* (New York, NY: Viking Penguin, 1998).

10: *ibid.*

11: *ibid.*

Chapter Five:

12: Kenneth McGee, *Heads Up* (Watertown, Mass.: Harvard Business School Press, 2004).

Chapter Six:

13: *World Book Encyclopedia*, 2008: Vol. 6. The San Diego Natural History Museum: timeline.

14-17: *ibid.*

18: Peter Gammons, *Israel in Prophecy* (Santa Ana, Calif: TBN Books, Special Edition, 1992).

19: *ibid.*

20: F.F. Bruce, New American Standard Bible, Study Edition (New York, N.Y.: A.J. Holman Co.).

21-25: *ibid.*

Chapter Seven:

26: William J. Federer, *America's God and Country, Encyclopedia of Quotations* (St. Louis, Mo.: Amerisearch, 2000).

Chapter Eight:

27: Craig Blomberg, *From Pentecost to Patmos* (Nashville, Tenn.: B&H, 2007).

28: *ibid.*

29: Craig Blomberg, *Jesus and the Gospels: An Introduction and Survey* (Nashville, Tenn.: B&H, 1997, 2009).

30-37: *ibid.*

38: Peter Gammons, *Israel in Prophecy* (Santa Ana, Calif: TBN Books, Special Edition, 1992).

39: D. James Kennedy, *Messiah: Prophecies Fulfilled* (Ft. Lauderdale, FL: Coral Ridge Ministries, 2003).

40-42: *ibid.*

43: Lee Strobel, *The Case for Christ* (Grand Rapids, Mich: Zondervan, 1998).

44: Quoted in: Lee Strobel, *The Case for Christ* (Grand Rapids, Mich: Zondervan, 1998).

Breinigsville, PA USA
01 February 2010
231703BV00006B/2/P